THE NEW MAN

30 PRINCIPLES FOR REAL LIFE TRANSFORMATION

BY: JOSEPH G. KING

Table of Contents

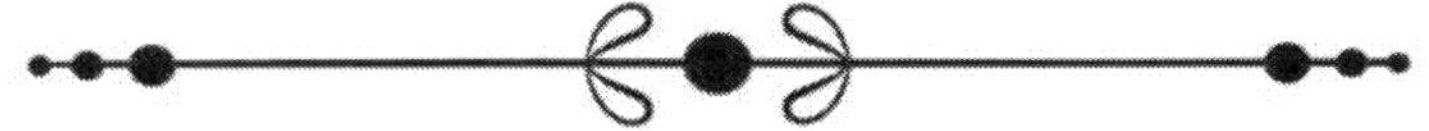

Foreword

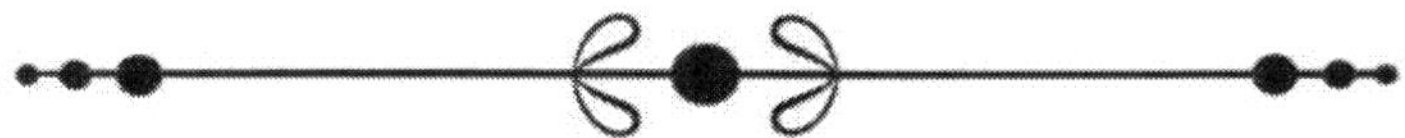

As a Spiritual Father to Joseph, I'm so proud to watch him transform right before my eyes. Sometimes our destiny takes us through a series of life challenges just like Joseph in the Bible days, our journey is filled with pits that we created for ourselves or pits that were God ordained. Sometimes our pits are there because of favor over our lives that we didn't see. Either way, God was orchestrating Joseph's life to fulfill his purpose and will. I have watched Joseph in his journey ever since he was a teenager until now a mature man. He epitomizes a person who went through the process of transformation. Transformation is the process of transforming or changing the outward form, the change in character or condition. It is a metamorphosed into something else. I First watched his personal transformation into a new creation in Christ. **2 Corinthians 5:17** says "Therefore, if anyone is in Christ, he is a new creation. The old has passed away; behold, the new has come." Secondly, I watched his mind transformation.

Romans 12:2 says "Do not be conformed to this world, but be transformed by the renewal of your mind, that by testing you may discern what is the will of God, what is good and acceptable and perfect. Here, transformation involves a change in thinking, aligning one's thoughts with God's will. Thirdly, I have watched his transformation from a convicted felon into a husband who loves his wife. Fourthly, I have watched his transformation into a loving father and lastly, into an author/businessman. I believe that God has taught Joseph these 30 PRINCIPLES FOR REAL LIFE TRANSFORMATION. This book will truly bless and enrich your life as you apply the principles that he learned by walking through his life journey. Although transformation is not easy, it is necessary. Be prepared to be transformed into "THE NEW MAN".

Bishop Willie C. Butts
Faith & Power Church

Preface

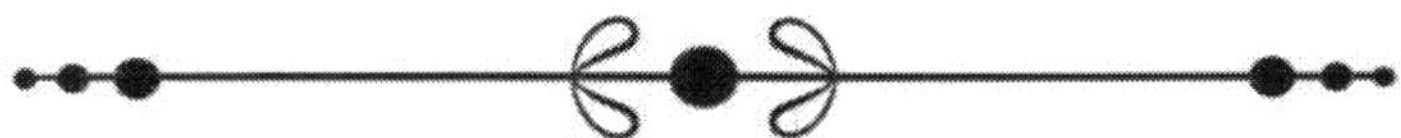

The journey of transformation is one of the most challenging yet rewarding experiences one can undertake. It requires a deep commitment to change, a willingness to confront the parts of ourselves that are difficult to face, and the courage to step into the unknown. In writing "The New Man: 30 Principles to Real Life Transformation," my goal is to share the principles and lessons that have guided me through my transformation.

This book is not just a collection of ideas; it is a testament to the power of faith, resilience, and the support of loved ones. Each principle outlined in this book is rooted in real-life experiences and biblical wisdom and in the things of Jesus Christ, my Lord and Savior. They are designed to help you navigate the complexities of life and emerge as a stronger, more fulfilled individual. As you read through these pages, you will find personal stories that highlight the struggles and triumphs of my journey. These stories are shared with the hope that they will resonate with you and provide encouragement and insight as you embark on your path of transformation. The principles discussed are practical and actionable, intended to help you make meaningful changes in your life.

One of the core messages of this book is the importance of recognizing the need for change and taking intentional steps toward that change. Whether it's building a support network, setting and achieving goals, or learning to say no, each principle is a building block that contributes to the foundation of a transformed life.

I want to emphasize the significance of spiritual guidance in this journey. For me, faith in God has been the anchor that has kept me grounded and provided direction when the path was unclear. It is my hope that you, too, will find strength and guidance in your faith as you work through these principles.

Transformation is not a one-time event but a continuous process of growth and self-improvement. As you apply these principles, you will discover new aspects of yourself, develop healthier relationships, and create a life that aligns with your true purpose. Thank you for allowing me to share my journey with you. I pray that this book will be a valuable resource and a source of inspiration as you pursue your transformation.

Joseph Permenter

Acknowledgements

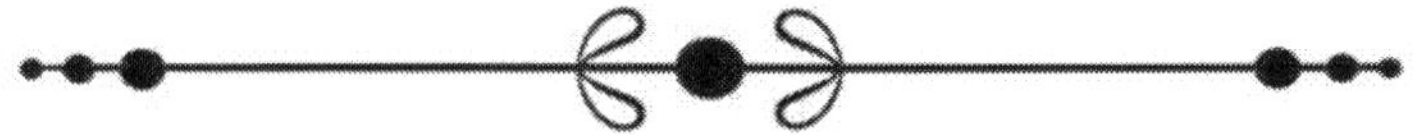

First and foremost, I would like to thank my Lord and Savior Jesus Christ for the opportunity to share my life experiences with whomever He allows to read this book. A mere man of many mistakes, but the grace of God has allowed me to continue to press toward the mark. I thank my wife (Chanta' Permenter) and kids (Duke, Azariya, Qi'Yaunna, and Calvin Joseph Permenter Jr) for being there for me through thick and thin, regardless of what obstacles came our way; we faced it together. To my mom and dad (Maurice and Mary Permenter). To my brothers (Maurice, Denante, Marcus, and Marvis Permenter). My one and only sister (Chiquita McNeil) I appreciate all the support throughout years of hardship, good and unpleasant times, I love you all.

To my church family that has been there my entire life through it all. Bishop Willie and Prophetess Wilma Butts (Who prophesied this book years ago in front of an open audience). I cannot say enough about your leadership. I do not know where I would be in life without you. And to Colossia Butts, (@colossiabutts on all social media platforms) there is no other Life Coach that I know who can fill your shoes. I would not be a writer-entertainer today if you had not pushed me to do so. I will forever be in debt to your service. Thank you!

Travis J. Ayers, for all the time and effort you put into making this book happen. Craig Frazier (Chickenman), for hearing me out while sitting in prison when this book was only a thought. Ronnie White, for being a long-time friend, standing in the gap for me always. (Brother in Christ). Again, to my wife who had to endure hardships because of my bad choices in life, this is for you. This is for every woman who has to deal with the man that's been shaped by his environment. We can only operate in the capacity that we know how to, after this, no more excuses. For the women, this is a guide to helping him jump-start his life for the better. The purpose of this book is to reach back and help any and everyone who has been imprisoned mentally, whether you've been incarcerated or not. I truly believe prison starts in the mind.

Prayerfully, this book reaches and helps millions shift their life through these principles. Through this book, you will learn how to navigate through life's lessons and tough times with a strategic mindset and understand what to expect. Knowing is half the battle. I genuinely believe if you apply these principles, you will shift your life completely. Always remember, transformation is ongoing; you will always need to use these principles. You should never feel as if you've obtained it all and continue to work on yourself for the rest of your life.....

About the Note to Spouse: The note to spouse is really me expressing the way I felt about needing my spouse during my times of transformation. For me, my wife is the biggest part of my change process. It is something about a woman and her influence. When a woman is in her perfect position, the results are undeniable. God ordained marriages and when 2 people agree, there is nothing that can stop them, NOTHING!

Genesis 2:18-25

THE NEW MAN GENERATION PRESENCE "The New Man" (30 principles to real-life transformation)

Colossians 3:9-10 9 Lie not one to another, seeing that ye have put off the old man with his deeds: 10and have put on the new man, which is renewed in knowledge after the image of him that created him.

"We as men must find more creative ways to make ends meet versus enslaving ourselves with a life of crime." (13th amendment)—Joseph G. King

2 Chronicles 7:14: "If My people who are called by My name will humble themselves, and pray and seek My face, and turn from their wicked ways, then I will hear from heaven, and will forgive their sin and heal their land."

Introduction

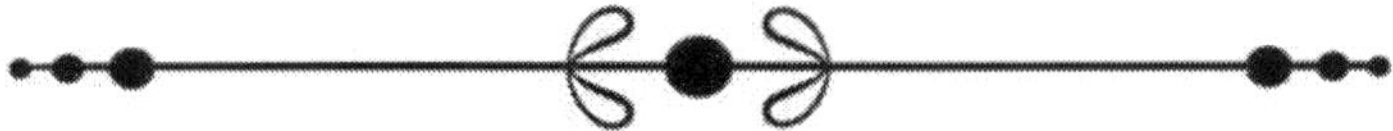

Welcome to "The New Man", a guide to real-life transformation built on thirty principles. My name is Joseph G. King Permenter. Through this book, I aim to share the wisdom I have gathered through personal experience, struggles, and, my journey to transformation. This book is designed to help you navigate through the complexities of life, offering practical advice and spiritual guidance. Whether you've faced hardships, made mistakes, or are simply seeking a better path, these principles are here to guide you.

Transformation is not a one-time event; it's an ongoing process. I have experienced many difficult moments fighting the old man to the point of becoming new, incarcerated physically and mentally through this process with no direction on how to transform my life. Each chapter of this book delves into a specific principle that has played a crucial role in my life and can do the same for you. From understanding the power of your words, to the importance of setting goals. Each principle is a stepping stone on the path to becoming a better version of yourself.

Throughout this book, you will find quick stories from my life that illustrate these principles in action. These stories are meant to give real-world examples of how applying these principles can lead to profound change. Additionally, each chapter includes practical exercises and tips to help you incorporate these principles into your daily life.

Remember, transformation is a journey, not a destination. It requires dedication, self-reflection, and a willingness to change. By committing to these principles and applying them consistently, you can achieve the life you want and deserve. Let us embark on this journey together and transform into "The New Man" that God has destined us to be.

Chapter 1

Recognizing the Need for Change

1 Corinthians 13:11 *When I was a child, I understood as a child. I thought as a child: but when I became a man, I put away childish things.*

Jesus looked at them and said, "With man, this is impossible, but with God, all things are possible." ***(Matthew 19:26)***

Quick Story:
The Turning Point

My journey of transformation began with the stark realization something had to change. Growing up in the challenging environment of Broward County, Florida, I was surrounded by drug dealers and athletes. These were the only role models I saw and naturally, I aspired to be like them. The allure of quick success through the streets seemed far more attainable than the uncertain path of becoming a professional athlete.

As a child, I was a straight 'A' student and an exceptional football player. I loved school and thrived in sports. However, the rewards I received for scoring touchdowns came from men who represented success in my eyes, the street dealers. They drove nice cars, wore nice clothes, and seemed to have it all together. This distorted view of success led me down a path I believe was right, even though it was fraught with danger and illegality.

By the age of fourteen, I was already hustling in different states. In 1999, my life took a turn when I was arrested for trafficking cocaine and sentenced to eighteen months in prison in the state of North Carolina. This harsh reality check was a pivotal moment. My words had power. I had often said I would not go to jail for anything small, and indeed, my prophecy came true in the worst way possible.

It was not until much later in life that I realized something needed to change. Transformation seemed impossible because I could not see any other way of life. This belief system, shaped by my exposure to the streets and my environment, kept me trapped in a cycle of drug dealing, strip clubs, gambling, and violence. It took years of mistakes, learning who I was, and understanding the power of change to begin my journey of transformation.

One of the most significant moments in my life was me realizing that there had to be more to life. I was deep into a lifestyle that was leading me nowhere. I remember sitting in a prison cell, reflecting on my life choices. It was then that I understood that if I did not change, I would continue down a path of destruction. This realization was the first step towards my transformation. I had to acknowledge my mistakes, accept responsibility for my actions, and decide that I wanted a better life for myself and my family.

New Man Principle #1: Recognizing the Need for Change

Change begins with recognition. You cannot change what you do not acknowledge. **Proverbs 4:7** says, "Wisdom is the principal thing; therefore, get wisdom: and with all thy getting, get understanding." Understanding your current state and recognizing the need for change is crucial for transformation.

Self-awareness is the foundation of personal growth. It involves looking at your life honestly and finding areas that require improvement. This process can be uncomfortable, but it is necessary for growth. Without recognizing the need for change, you will remain stagnant, repeating the same mistakes and missing opportunities for a better life.

Signs You Need A Change

Recognizing the need for change is the first step towards transformation. Some signs that show it is time to make a shift in your life.

Constant frustration: Frequent filling of frustration or anger might indicate that something is not aligning with your true self.

Lack of fulfillment: Feeling unfulfilled or stuck in a rut often signals that you need to re-evaluate your path.

Physical and mental exhaustion: Chronic stress and exhaustion can be an indicator that your current lifestyle is unsustainable.

Repeating Negative Patterns: A cycle of negative

behaviors or outcomes is a strong sign that changes are necessary.

Loss Of Passion: When activities and goals that once excited you no longer bring joy, it's time to explore new avenues.

Steps To Recognize the Need for Change

1. **Self-Reflection:** Spend time in prayer and meditation, asking God to reveal areas in your life that need change.
2. **Honest Evaluation:** Take an honest look at your life and identify patterns of behavior that are holding you back.
3. **Seek Feedback:** Ask trusted friends, family members, or mentors for their honest feedback about areas you need to improve.
4. **Set Goals:** Determine what you want to achieve and what changes are necessary to reach those goals.
5. **Commit to Change:** Make a commitment to yourself and to God that you will pursue the changes needed for your transformation.

The Importance of Seeking Help:

Do not be afraid to seek help. Sometimes, recognizing the need for change is not enough; you need guidance on how to continue. Seeking counsel from godly individuals, such as pastors, mentors, or counselors, can provide you with the support and wisdom needed to navigate your transformation journey.

The Cost of Staying the Same:

Staying in a situation that no longer serves you can be incredibly costly, both in tangible and intangible ways.

1. **Emotional Toll:** Remaining in an unfulfilling situation can lead to increased anxiety, depression, and a general sense of dissatisfaction.
2. **Lost Opportunities:** Stagnation often means missing out on potential growth and opportunities that could significantly improve your life.
3. **Health Issue:** Chronic stress can manifest in physical health problems, including high blood pressure, heart disease, and a weakened immune system.
4. **Strained Relationship:** Personal and professional relationships can suffer when you are not living authentically and are constantly unhappy.
5. **Regret:** One of the most significant costs of not changing is the regret of not having lived up to your full potential.

Practical Tips and Exercises

Exercise 1:

Self-Reflection Journal: Keep a journal where you document your thoughts, feelings, and observations about your life. Reflect on areas where you feel stuck or dissatisfied and write about why you think change is necessary.

Exercise 2:

Honest Conversations: Have a candid conversation with someone you trust. Ask for their perspective on areas in your life that may need change.

NOTE TO SPOUSE:

Supporting your spouse in recognizing the need for change is vital. Encourage them to self-reflect and be open to feedback. Be patient and understanding as they embark on their journey of transformation. Your support and encouragement can make a significant difference in their willingness and ability to change.

Chapter 2

Finding Your Anchor (Higher Power)

Importance of having a higher power
Matthew 7:24-26 (The wise and the foolish builder)

After realizing that you need change, the next principle, which is most important to transforming your life, is needing that anchor to sustain you during this process. Change can be simple by making small adjustments, but transformation is something greater; something permanent. We all change several things in our lives many times over, but to transform and sustain that change mindset, it's essential to be anchored and bolted down on a solid foundation.

When building a house or any type of structure, the foundation must be laid properly. If that foundation is rocky, the structure will be suspect and may not stand the test of time. Your willpower alone is not enough. I have been through so much that when I hear someone say they have strong will-power, I chuckle and watch them make countless mistakes because they think that will-power is all they need.

Think about some of the things you have tried to change in the past. Before you knew it, you were right back in the cycle of things you worked hard to change. Some changes last longer than others, but eventually, they too fall short. I have news for you, it's time to realize that you need help.

As for me, there are countless times I made real efforts to change some things, and deep down inside, it was a genuine effort. It always starts off good, and you are full of burning desire to get it done. But at some point, along the way, you get sidetracked. However, I can assure you there is a way that will keep you anchored and grounded on your way to transforming your life. Not perfect, (human perfection is a myth), but you will be transformed and unrecognizable by those who thought they knew you.

I can only share my experiences in this book, nothing more, nothing less. I may mention experiences I know of occasionally, but, this is my reality that I speak about.

Quick Story:

There was a time I smoked cigars and Black & Mild's. It eventually became an expensive and unhealthy habit. Those of you who have tried to quit smoking can feel me when I say the struggle is real. It is almost impossible to do it on your own. Will-power alone will allow you to go weeks and sometimes months, without smoking. But for some reason, I would always end up picking that habit back up, not understanding how and why it was defeating me. I thought I was a strong-willed person. My father-in-law and I (Jerry Mike Perry) spoke all the time about quitting smoking. He was a smoker too but could not shake it.

However, I now have a permanent solution that will last a lifetime if you allow it to and that solution is as solid as it gets. No, it was not a nicotine patch, chewing gum, or E cigarettes; nothing against any of those. But it is just not the anchor I am referring to. That anchor that works for me is none other than our Lord and Savior Jesus Christ, who has carried me throughout this transformation process by prayer and fasting. **(Matthew 17:21)**

It was a normal Sunday service and church was going on as usual. After the word was presented, there was an altar call. The Speaker asks those struggling with addiction to come up. Yes, I was struggling with addiction and could not shake it. Just to give you a heads-up, if you are struggling with something, you're not alone. Many people, including Christians, struggle with addiction. My Bishop (Willie Butts) call it, “Saved but Struggling”. You may be surprised with how many people who are sitting in church struggling with some type of addiction, but this is my reasonable service to share these experiences so you too can be delivered and transformed with no shame or pride understanding that we all need HIM!

Moving forward as the presider continued, I felt the pull to go up. Everything is done in God's timing, and timing is important to us all. Time alone ripens the fruit on the tree. If the timing is off, it is considered premature. Jesus himself understood this, which is why you can catch him biblically making statements such as, “My hour has not come” **(JOHN 2:4).**

This is Jesus understanding the importance of timing. Not saying that things would not take place, it is just the timing of the actual event. It is already done; we must catch up with God's timing.

Back to the story…..

At this time, I was meditating, I felt the pull to go up and get prayer. That pull represented God's timing. Sure enough, I went up, hands lifted, mind on healing, expecting the move of God. The very next thing that took place is evidence of why I believe this very day. (One of many spiritual experiences that I will talk about throughout this book). As the service went on, I was standing there meditating, and suddenly, I felt the impact of a rushing wind come over me. My mouth opened, and it felt like when you are at the dentist, and they use a dental suction tool to suck up saliva while they are working, like sluuuuuuuuuuuuuurp. The Lord was removing the smoke taste out of my mouth. I slowly looked around to see if anyone else saw what just happened, but everyone was in their own world. Since then, it was easy to keep a smoke-free life. That is something I could not have done on my own. It was that anchor that helped me shift my life, and the timing of it was the time that the heavens had set forth. Everything before that would have not yielded the same results.

The anchor I now have in the Lord allows me not only to change things, but to transform into the man I was once created to be without all the learned negativity that once consumed my life. I'm not saying you can't make small adjustments; those small adjustments are needed to create a changed lifestyle. But to sustain it, you will 100% at some point need an anchor to hold you in place. If you do not know the Lord and Savior (Yeshua A.K.A. Jesus Christ), here is an open invitation to be saved. It is a gift for any and everyone who is willing to come forth, no matter your past or present mistakes. If I can call on him to hold me down, so can you. **(Romans 10:9)**

Father, I pray that whoever encounters this book, allow their lives to be transformed. Not just a temporary change that they are used to but provide a permanent solution for them to sustain a lifestyle of relying on you and not themselves in the name of Jesus!

The New Man Principle #2: Finding an Anchor

To truly transform, you need to find a higher power—Jesus Christ. **Proverbs 3:5-6** says, "Trust in the Lord with all thine heart; and lean not unto thine own understanding. In all thy ways acknowledge him, and he shall direct thy paths."

Your relationship with God is the cornerstone of your transformation. Having a higher power gives you a sense of purpose and direction. It provides you with the strength to overcome challenges and the wisdom to make better decisions. This principle emphasizes the importance of developing a deep, personal relationship with God and allowing Him to guide you through your transformation.

Building a Relationship with God

1. **Prayer:** Communicate with God regularly. Prayer is your direct line to Him and is essential for building a strong relationship.
2. **Bible Study:** Spend time reading and studying the

Bible. It is God's word and will to provide you with the guidance and wisdom you need.

3. **Fellowship:** Surround yourself with other believers who can support and encourage you in your walk with Christ.
4. **Worship:** Worship God in spirit and truth. Worship helps you to focus on Him and strengthens your relationship.
5. **Obedience:** Follow God's commandments and live according to His word. Obedience is a key component of a strong relationship with God.

The Importance of Faith

Faith is believing in what you cannot see and trusting in God's plan for your life. **Hebrews 11:1** says, "Now faith is the substance of things hoped for, the evidence of things not seen."

Faith is essential for transformation because it allows you to trust God's process, even when you don't understand it.

Practical Tips and Exercises

Exercise 1:

Daily Devotions: Start your day with a devotional time, reading the Bible, and praying.

Exercise 2:

Join a Bible Study Group: Participate in a Bible study group to deepen your understanding of God's word and build community with other believers.

Exercise 3:

Worship Playlist: Create a worship playlist and spend time listening to and singing songs that glorify God.

Exercise 4:

Scripture Memorization: Memorize key scriptures that speak to your heart and meditate on them throughout the day.

NOTE TO SPOUSE:

Whether you are a wife, girlfriend, boyfriend, or husband, give your partner grace when it comes to mistakes and flaws because it is the same grace that God gives us all. Transformation needs to be supported by the ones you love the most. You wonder why things keep going back to the same thing as a revolving door, it is because the anchor has not been attached to the foundation. Be a good spouse and get spiritual leadership and guidance. Be patient through prayer.

Chapter 3

Building A Support Group

The Power Of Positive Influence

Your environment is crucial to your identity. When it comes to shifting and transforming your life, it is important where you are located and who you are around. Remember the phrase, "Birds of a feather flock together."

This holds true, and you will always hear me say that. Unfortunately, we often do not believe it until we have experienced it most of our lives. Me included. I can remember hanging around a certain group of people growing up, and no matter how different I thought I was, I was still considered one of them. It was tough because they did not have the best reputation, and I pleaded my case all the time to show others that, that was not who I was, but to no avail.

The Bible says that bad company corrupts good character, and character is everything. (More on character throughout this book). Bottom line, you are who you surround yourself with. My father used to say, "Son, if you hang around four broke brothers, you're destined to be the fifth."

So true. The best thing you can do at this point in life is to sit back and elevate your circle of friends. Do not be afraid to cut bait with those who do not look like where you are going.

Different Rooms

My Bishop, Willie Butts, will always say "you have to see it before you see it." Getting to know me, you will find out that I grew up in the hood. I ran the streets all my life, it is what I knew, and the people I hung around did the same things I did. It was my lifestyle and my ceiling. I was stuck and trapped. The only way I could even begin to see something different was to shift my circle of friends. Once I did that, I began to realize that life is bigger than the four corners I was used to. Only then, I could be strategic about whom I surrounded myself with. I can now see it before I saw it.

Fast-forward from my new circle, I could now form a support group that was going in the direction I was going in and living the lifestyle I wanted to live. It is a shift. On the flip side, not all old friends want to see you change or shift. It is not that they do not like you, it is simply because they are currently in the same stuck state that you were once in. By the grace of God, you are now thinking about change. If you are hungry for it, God will fill you up to the capacity of your hunger and thirst **(Matthew 5:6).**

Meanwhile, your old friends would not understand this phase because they have never seen you in this light before. Do not be surprised if most of them don't support the new you. It is ok because not everyone will go where you are going. It is up to you to discern those who will support the change. Allow yourself to be held accountable by those who love you most. Now, this is not an overnight gig, it is an ongoing process. So, you will have to be prepared for the long ride.

I can remember when I first set out to change some things in my life, I had this one friend who would make fun of my progress all the time. It started out funny, but then I realized the seriousness of his words. For me to shift, I had to eventually separate myself from that individual because he was shaking up my change process with his words. He just did not understand that a person like me, so rooted in the streets, could try to get out; especially with the level of popularity I had. So, it was obvious that this individual could no longer take up space in my life because he was not a supporter in my change process.

Now, not all friends are like that. You have some that will respect your decision to shift and protect you from the old environment. These are the ones you can have minimum contact with, knowing that there is a separation and a difference in the direction you are traveling in. It starts off hard but gains momentum as you become victorious in certain areas. This journey must be spiritual because you are going to need divine direction from above to even pull this off. As for me, I started to seek help and support from my family and church family because I did not know how to pull this off on my own. My advice to you is to start with family and church family because they will usually support change automatically, as they did not support your current lifestyle in the first place. They are typically genuine about seeing your shifts, these individuals are where you start your support group and if you do not have a church home, my advice is to find one and plant yourself. When that is done, form a support group at once.

The New Man Principle #3

Support Group

Maintaining Support Group

1. **Communicate Openly:** Honest and open communication is the foundation of any healthy relationship. Share your thoughts, feelings, and needs clearly, and listen actively to others.
2. **Set boundaries:** Respect each other's boundaries and understand that everyone has different limits and needs. Setting and respecting boundaries prevents misunderstandings and keeps a healthy balance.
3. **Show Appreciation:** Express gratitude for the support you receive and appreciation for the efforts of your support group members, fosters positive interaction and strengthens your bond.
4. **Be reliable:** Consistency and reliability build trust. Try to be there for your support group members when they need you and allow yourself to follow through on your commitments.
5. **Encourage Growth:** Support each other's growth and development. Celebrate success together and provide constructive feedback when necessary.

Real Life

To illustrate the impact of surrounding yourself with a support group, here are some real-life examples from me of the way I transformed my life with the help of positive influence.

Being in the streets, I was trapped in a lifestyle that offered no real future. My transformation began when I started to shift my circle of friends. It was the support from my family and church family, which provided the encouragement and accountability I needed. My wife, who hated my negative lifestyle, became my number one supporter. Her genuine support was crucial because she was most affected by my bad decisions. My kids also motivated me to be better, as I wanted to be more active and present in their lives.

Again, another important wave of support came from my church family, especially my leaders, Bishop Willie C. Butts and Overseer Wilma Butts of my church home Faith and Power, also with their daughter, Colossia Butts. They have been prayer warriors and have supported me through every phase of my life. Colossia has been a major influence, encouraging me to see myself in a different light and unlocking potential I did not even know I had. I have been part of this ministry, Faith and Power Church since I was a little boy. They have always supported my immediate family, even when I was going through my incarceration period. My church family was always there, praying and speaking over my life, helping me to get to a certain level, even indulging in my marriage. They kept me lifted in prayer during each of my prison bids, and they did not once give up on me.

Hebrew 3:13 encourages us to support one another daily. I urge you, the reader, to get into your rightful place. God has appointed certain leaders who can unlock your destiny. As my leaders would say, "Not everyone has the key to unlock your destiny." It is your job to discern and find good leaders who can help you transform your life. Who is in your support group? Who are you following?

NOTE TO SPOUSE:

Be his support. Me, I would rather my wife be my number one supporter.

Genesis 2:18 reveals that God thought it was not good for a man to be alone, so he created a suitable helper. Spouse, be his help. Remember your position, even when things are not favorable. You need each other's support first.

Chapter 4

Building Healthy Relationships

Quick Story:
Shifting My Environment

This principle goes hand in hand with Principle #3. With the mentality I had, just like I mentioned in Principle #1, I could not see the problem in my lifestyle because it is all I was used to. However, once I was forced to get a job by my work release status, through favor I landed a job where I started working around millionaires. It was then that I learned different strategies on how to make money, which eventually shifted my mindset. I realized that I was more than just a drug dealer or a street dude.

I was able to unlock some of my real gifts and potentials that I didn't know I had. Had I not shifted my environment, who knows where I would be today.

I didn't get my first real job until age thirty, working around a room full of people making legal money. I realized that I belonged in that world just as much as they did. By the grace of God, I fit right in with no education, no job experience, and no resume; Favor was all I had and all I needed.

Bottom line, when I shifted my circle, my life changed for the better. The thing I learned about the circle of friends is that once you shift your mind, you can look back and see your old circle doing the same things over and over. As for me, it opened an entirely different world.

News flash: Your talents and gifts are being buried because of your circle of friends. You are limiting yourself, going through the motions, only existing, not maximizing your life potential—all because of who you are around. One of the things that worked for me was that I stopped giving old friends access to me. I changed my phone number and stopped coming around. If you do not have my number, and I am not being seen, how can you access me?

Now let us take a rabbit trail and talk social media, that is another form of friends or relationships, checking your usage will be wise, for an example, it can be extremely negative if you do not strategize while using it. It will also have you interacting with people that aren't going where you are going. I challenge you to stay off social media and watch how your life starts changing. You could be spending too much time with the circle of social media friends who are making money while you keep up with their lives. It is another circle of unknown friends that you must separate from. Especially if you're not established.

The New Man Principle #4:

Building Healthy Relationships-Evaluate Your Circle of

Friends.

"Do not be deceived, bad company corrupts good character." **(1 Corinthians 15:33)**

AGAIN, DO NOT FORGET, "Birds of a feather flock together."

Your environment and the people you spend the most time with will influence you; whether for good or bad. It's vitally important to take inventory of whom you allow in your space, especially when seeking transformation. I have always had a leadership spirit. But even I recognized that no matter how much you try to deny it, you will be affected by who's in your everyday circle. This principle works both negatively and positively, so keep that in mind when you open your space to certain people.

Reflecting on my experience, I realized that I didn't do certain things unless I was around specific people. It's something about this principle that holds truth. For example, I had a friend as a teenager who loved to chase women. While I was involved in many things; (mainly hustling). Whenever I was around him, I found myself around different women all day because that was what he liked to do. When I wasn't around him, I wasn't around different women because it was not my character. It was simply his company that influenced me.

The same goes for another friend who liked to drink. I would not think about drinking until he came around. The first thing he would say is, "Bro, let's get a bottle".

From there, we would be at the liquor store. I would drink

but not like him. Once with him, you better believe we were heading to the store or club to get drinks. It is the company that causes you to respond differently based on whom you're around at that time. This principle also works positively. If you change your negative circle of friends and surround yourself with positive energy and people who are productive and making moves, you'll pick up on that frequency and become a move-maker as well. Take the time to stop and really look at who you are spending the most time with and ask yourself, (How is this relationship affecting my lifestyle?).

Steps to Improve Existing Relationships

Not all relationships are beyond repair. With effort and communication, many relationships can be improved. Here are some steps to help improve existing relationships:

1. **Open Communication:** Address issues openly and honestly. Express your feelings and listen to the other person's perspective without judgment.

2. **Set Boundaries:** Set up clear boundaries to ensure mutual respect. Communicate your limits and expectations clearly.

3. **Practice Empathy:** Try to understand the other person's feelings and viewpoints. Empathy fosters deeper connections and mutual respect.

4. **Seek Compromise:** Healthy relationships often require compromise. Be willing to find middle ground and make concessions when necessary.

5. **Invest Time and Effort:** Relationships require time and effort to flourish. Make a conscious effort to spend quality time together and show appreciation for each other.

Building New, Positive Relationships:

Building new, positive relationships is essential for personal growth and happiness. Here are some tips to help you build and maintain healthy relationships:

1. **Be Authentic:** Be yourself and be honest about your values, interests, and goals. Authenticity attracts like-minded individuals.
2. **Join Communities:** Take part in groups or communities that align with your interests and values. This could be clubs, volunteer organizations, or online forums.
3. **Show Interest in Others**: Take the time to get to know others and show genuine interest in their lives. Ask questions and listen actively.
4. **Be Reliable:** Consistency and reliability build trust. Be dependable and keep your commitments.
5. **Support and Encourage:** Offer support and encouragement to others. Celebrate their successes and be there for them during challenging times.

Practical Tips and Exercises

Exercise 1:

Relationship Audit: Take some time to evaluate your current relationships. Write down the names of the people you interact with regularly and assess the quality of each relationship. Identify any toxic relationships and think about ways to address or distance yourself from them.

Exercise 2:

Building Boundaries: Reflect on your boundaries in relationships. Write down areas where you feel your boundaries are being crossed and think about ways to communicate these boundaries to the people involved. Practice setting and maintaining these boundaries in your interactions.

Exercise 3:

Gratitude Journal: Start a gratitude journal focused on your relationships. Each day, write down at least one thing you appreciate about the people in your life. This practice can help you focus on the positive aspects of your relationships and foster a deeper sense of connection and appreciation.

Exercise 4:

Empathy Practice: Choose a person in your life with whom you want to strengthen your relationship. Spend some time putting yourself in their shoes and reflecting on their perspective. Write down what you think their feelings and motivations might be. Use this understanding to approach your next interaction with them with greater empathy.

NOTE TO SPOUSE:

If you are a wife, girlfriend, husband, or boyfriend, evaluate the time you spend with other friends and on social media. Spend that time with each other and build on your future. Don't be the one that lays in bed for hours watching someone else make moves. Most importantly, stop giving people easy access to contact you or reach you. You are being fooled, and you don't even know it. You're basing your life on what you see on social media, and most of it is fake news. Evaluate your physical circle and your social media circle and spend time working on your projects. Produce your own ideas and stop being a follower of what you see.

Chapter 5

Consistently Checking Yourself

Quick Story:

Redefining Roles

Growing up with four brothers, my dad raised us in a certain way. He taught us to be men, but we were not allowed to do certain things, like clean up. Sweeping, mopping, or washing dishes was off-limits because it was considered a woman's work. A man was supposed to take out the garbage, cut grass, etc. As I got older, I realized that I enjoyed cooking and cleaning. Washing dishes became a part of cooking for me. After discovering that about myself, I had to check myself and let go of what I was taught.

Another good point is that what works for one household may not work for another. I have friends who believe a man is supposed to do certain things, and the same goes for women. Once I took inventory of myself and my household, I realized our setup was different from the average household. I learned that I enjoyed certain things so much that it didn't matter what the next man did. According to most of my friends, my wife should cook more, but that didn't work for us, and that's all that matters. Just for the record, my wife loves to cook and clean, but I also love to give her a break occasionally and I'm fine with that, again that's what works for us....

If you're not careful, you'll base your life on others and eventually find out you're forcing a lifestyle that doesn't work for you. Spend time with yourself, discovering what you like and dislike. Share it with your significant other so you both can get on the same page. Self-inventory should be frequent because what you liked years ago may not be what you like today. Seasons change, and so do people.

Lamentations 3:40: 'Let us examine our ways in testing come and let us return to the Lord'

Examining your ways is a well-rounded approach to self-inventory. It helps you to really examine yourself, your character, and your intentions. Occasionally, we find ourselves wanting a certain lifestyle based on what others have, only to discover we don't even like those things. All it is, is a fad based on what is popular.

Coming up in the hood, many things took place because it was what was popular at the moment. You may want things that you don't really like but do it anyway because others do it or just to say you did it. For years, I realized I was considerably basic when it came to fashion. I had moments of trying to fit in, but I felt extremely uncomfortable in the process. As a teenager, whenever we went shopping, I would always desire basic things and stay away from what was popular. A good friend of mine used to say I didn't have taste, but as I got older, I realized

I did have taste, it just was different from the norm.

I was not a huge fan of fashion at all, even when making money to buy expensive things. It wasn't in my mind to do so, and whenever I tried to do it, I felt uncomfortable. Until this day, I have never bought a Gucci belt or Louis Vuitton for myself. I have bought them for my wife because she wanted certain things at that time, but even she wasn't over the top with that stuff. Personally, I was never into all of that, and that's okay. I like Honda's, Toyota's, and Lexus will be my luxury car choice, (not a Beemer Benz or Bentley). For me, those are the things I like, and it's ok to know what you like and not base your life or desires on what's popular. I'm confident in my skin. I like things like Reeboks and Hard Bottom shoes. It doesn't matter whether it's popular or not, it's what I like. I've learned throughout the years to be ok with myself, and that only came after really learning who I am.

I am a leader, not a follower. Leaders set the pace, and they are not manipulated by what others do. A leader will do what he feels is right, no matter what. So, study yourself, take inventory, perform self check-ups often. Meditate on your heart's desires and find out what you really like, not what's popular. Always check yourself, it's easier than trying to be someone else.

The New Man Principle #5:

Consistently Check Yourself (Self Inventory)

"Check your character and your intent daily: 'But the things that come out of a person's mouth come from the heart, and these defile them.'" **(Matthew 15:17-19)**

Self-inventory is vital for transformation. It involves regularly assessing your thoughts, actions, and motives, to gain more profound insights into yourself. This practice, often called a self-check-up, is essential for shaping your world and understanding your true self. By examining yourself, you can uncover hidden aspects of your character and discover what truly drives you.

Techniques for Regular Self-Assessment

Taking consistent self-inventory requires adopting various self-assessment techniques. Here are some effective methods:

1. **Journaling**: Writing down your thoughts and experiences regularly can help you process your emotions and reflect on your actions. Journaling allows you to track your progress and identify recurring themes or issues.

2. **Mindfulness Meditation:** Practicing mindfulness helps you stay present and aware of your thoughts and feelings. It encourages you to see your mind without judgment, fostering a more profound understanding of yourself.

3. **Feedback from Others:** Seeking feedback from trusted friends, family, or mentors can offer valuable insights into your behavior and areas for improvement. Be open to constructive criticism and use it as a tool for growth.

4. **Self-Reflection Questions:** Ask yourself specific questions to prompt deeper thinking. Questions like, "What did I do well today? What could I have done

better? What did I learn from this experience?" These questions can guide your self-assessment process.

5. **Goal Setting and Review:** Regularly setting and reviewing your goals can help you stay focused and motivated. Assess your progress and make necessary adjustments to stay on track.

Adjusting Course When Needed

Life is full of unexpected twists and turns, and it's essential to be flexible and willing to adjust your course when needed. Here are some steps to help you adjust course effectively:

1. **Recognize the Need for Change:** Be aware of signs that indicate a need for change, such as feeling stuck, unfulfilled, or constantly encountering obstacles. Acknowledge that adjusting your course is a natural part of growth.

2. **Evaluate Your Current Path:** Take a good look at your current situation and identify what is not working. Reflect on your goals, values, and priorities to determine if they are still aligned with your actions.

3. **Set New Goals:** Based on your evaluation, set new, realistic goals that reflect your current aspirations and circumstances. Ensure that these goals are specific, measurable, achievable, relevant, and time-bound (SMART).

4. **Develop a Plan:** Create a detailed plan to achieve your new goals. Break down your goals into smaller,

manageable steps and set up a timeline for each.

5. **Act:** Implement your plan and take consistent action towards your new goals. Stay committed and adaptable, making further adjustments, as necessary.

Practical Tips and Exercises

Exercise 1:

Daily Journaling: Set aside 10–15 minutes each day to journal about your thoughts, feelings, and experiences. Focus on reflecting on your actions and identifying areas for improvement.

Exercise 2:

Mindfulness Meditation: Practice mindfulness meditation for 10–20 minutes daily. Sit in a quiet place, close your eyes, and focus on your breathing. Observe your thoughts and emotions without judgment.

Exercise 3:

Weekly Self-Reflection: At the end of each week, set aside time to reflect on your achievements and challenges. Ask yourself questions like, "What did I accomplish this week? What challenges did I face? How can I improve next week?"

Exercise 4:

Monthly Goal Review: Review your goals at the end of each month. Assess your progress, celebrate your successes, and identify any obstacles. Adjust your goals and plans as needed to stay on track.

Exercise 5:

Seek Feedback: Repeatedly ask for feedback from trusted individuals in your life. Be open to their perspectives and use their insights to inform your self-assessment and growth.

NOTE TO SPOUSE:

We often spend too much time examining what others are doing and trying to shape our situation to that. We want our significant others to be like what we see on TV, rather than embracing who they truly are and pouring into their desires. Likewise, we are all guilty of it.

From this day forward, examine the things that you and your spouse like and build on that instead of comparing your lives to what you see. It's all fake news. Your life will transform, and you will be happy in your skin. Love your spouse for who they are and who God created them to be, not who you think they should be. It's ok to have role models, but love each other for who you are, and your lives will be peaceful.

"Know thyself by checking thyself."

Chapter 6

Accepting Feedback

Why feedback is crucial....

The New Man Principle #6:
Accepting Feedback (Genuine Feedback)

And let us consider how to stir up one another to love and good works, not neglecting to meet, as it is the habit of some, but encouraging one another, and all the more as you see the day drawing near **(Hebrew 10:24-25)**

On your path to transformation, it's not only important to have support and accountability, but also to accept genuine feedback from credible sources. Feedback can be tough to take in and apply to your everyday life. But once you've shaped your circle with people who share your vision and have your best interest at heart, their feedback can significantly influence your decision-making. Often, people are assigned to you who can see what you can't.

Personal Reflection:

When I was making my transition, a few people spoke into my life, and I knew they had my best interest at heart. My wife was the most critical and probably the hardest to listen to because of her direct delivery. Despite not always liking her approach, her feedback was meaningful and helpful. Had I listened to her sooner, I could have saved myself plenty of heartache because she often was spot on. That's another story for another book.

My leaders taught me that not everyone has the key to unlock things in your life but once you're connected to the right people, you have a free ride to bettering yourself. Accepting feedback from those who genuinely care about you can be life changing. (As I mentioned) My Church family and leaders are crucial in my change process. They applaud my success but also hold me accountable when needed. That feedback is essential because they want the best for me and want to see me walk in my purpose.

I have made some poor decisions in my life. Especially as I got older. At one point, I made some changes, and I was working on myself, a lot happened, and a lot went wrong, and I started walking backwards, indulging in things I had no business indulging in. When everything was exposed, facing those important people in my life whom I let down was one of the hardest things to do. They were going to tell me the truth, whether I liked it or not. It was hard at first, but when I came to myself, it was precisely what I needed to hear. I thank God for placing certain people in my life. Without them, I can't say where I would be today.

To my wife and family, also Church Family especially my leaders Bishop, Prophetess Butts and my sister and my Life Coach Colossia Butts, AGAIN! I love you all for the good, bad, and ugly feedback that had to help me transform my life for good.

How To Accept and Act on Feedback

1. **Be open and receptive:** Approach feedback with an open mind and a willingness to listen. Understanding that feedback is a tool for growth, not a personal attack.
2. **Listen Actively:** Pay attention to thc fccdback being given without interrupting or becoming defensive. Note if necessary to ensure you fully understand the points being made.
3. **Ask for clarification:** If any part of the feedback is unclear, ask for specific examples or further explanations. This helps ensure you accurately understand the feedback and its context.
4. **Reflect On the Feedback:** Take some time to reflect on the feedback before responding. Consider how it aligns with your perceptions and experiences.
5. **Develop An Action Plan:** Based on the feedback, create a plan to address the areas of improvement. Set specific, measurable goals and outline the steps it would take to achieve them.
6. **Implement Changes:** Put your action plan into practice

and make the necessary changes to your progress and adjust as needed.

7. **Seek Follow-up Feedback:** After making changes seek additional feedback to assess your progress. This will help you stay on track and continue improving.

Constructive VS Destructive Feedback

Understanding the difference between constructive and destructive feedback is crucial for personal growth. One builds you up while the other is to tear you down.

1. **Constructive Feedback:** This type of feedback is intended to help you improve. This is specific, actionable, and delivered with a positive intent. Constructive feedback focuses on behaviors and outcomes, not personal attributes. Example: 'I noticed that you often missed deadlines. You could benefit from better time management strategies, like setting interim goals and using a planner.'

2. **Destructive Feedback:** This type of feedback is often vague, negative, and not aimed at helping you improve. It can be personal, critical, and demotivating. Example: You're always late and unreliable.

BE SURE TO REQUEST FEEDBACK FROM RELIABLE SOURCES AND BE ABLE TO SEPARATE THE TWO TYPES.

NOTE TO SPOUSE:

Listen, the most important person in your life is your spouse, so it's crucial to treat each other as such. Often, we have negative outlooks on each other because of past hurts, but that needs to be changed today. Get a new vision of your spouse through faith. Be careful how you treat and criticize each other because it can make or break your relationship. I learned to be gentle and strategic when giving my wife feedback, and I've also learned to understand her feedback to me, even if it comes off harsh. Communicate and tell each other what you like and dislike and learn to accept that feedback and apply it to your daily lives.

Chapter 7

Being Open Minded

Balancing Open Mindedness with Wisdom

The New Man Principle #7:
Be Open Minded but Closed Minded to Foolishness

On the road to transformation, it's essential to be open-minded and coachable because you don't have all the answers. **Proverbs 15:32, Proverbs 19:20-29**, reminds us of the values of accepting wisdom and instructions. In life, there are certain things you miss out on when you fail to be open-minded, especially to those put in place to help you succeed. However, there are also ideas and influences that you need to be closed off to because it can hinder your growth, and you will see them from a mile away.

Staying focused on major decisions requires prayer, consistently talking to God, and using your discerning spirit to separate good decisions from God - inspired decisions. One thing I've learned on this journey is to hear everyone out because it costs you nothing. Only a fool answers a matter before he hears it. However, knowing when to shut things down is equally important. Know when to close your gates, meaning some things should not be allowed to enter your mind and heart.

Quick Story:

I set out to start a business and thought I had it all figured out. I didn't think I needed much help and was confident in my abilities. However, I was in over my head and on my way to a rude awakening, a real roller coaster ride. My ex-employer, (a multi-millionaire, may I mention), reached out to me to have a conversation about business. I was so stuck in my ways and in my feelings about something he did that I refused to sit down with him, one of the worst decisions that I've made in hindsight I should have sat down and heard what he had to offer. Being closed-minded cost me eventually. It would have cost me nothing to hear him out, and I could have benefited from his insight and experience.

Being Closed Minded to Negativity:

On the other hand, being closed-minded to negativity has also been beneficial. For example, I'm close to anything negative, rather it's a negative-minded person or a negative plan. Every so often, you know a person, or a plan is negative, yet you still follow through for some reason. You have to be ok with saying no and be comfortable with it. (That's another topic). Work on being closed-minded to what you know isn't right, your gut will alert you every single time.

Certain things are not allowed to hit my spirit. Occasionally, you must cut friends off mid-sentence to prevent them from planting negative seeds. Be mindful of what you allow to enter your heart in mind, as seeds are being planted whether you know it or not. This principle is essential, being open-minded can help you reach certain levels, but being close minded to foolishness is crucial to keeping your focus and direction. Stay away from negativity, don't even allow it to occupy your space.

Being close minded to certain things can save you a lot of heartache, just as being open-minded can lead to success. Here are some ways to avoid foolishness:

1. **Set Boundaries**: Establish clear personal boundaries that align with your values and goals. This helps you filter out ideas and influences that are not in your best interest.

2. **Seek Advice:** Consult trusted mentors, friends, or family members when faced with new ideas or decisions. Their perspectives can provide valuable insight and help you make informed choices.

3. **Evaluate Sources:** consider credibility and reliability of the sources of new information. Not all sources are trustworthy, so it's important to verify the authenticity of what you hear or read.

4. **Reflect on Past Experiences:** Learning from your past experiences and mistakes, reflecting on what has worked and what hasn't can guide you in making better decisions in the future.

Developing Critical Thinking Skills

Critical thinking is a crucial component of being open-minded yet discerning. It involves analyzing information, evaluating evidence, and making recent judgments.

NOTE TO SPOUSE:

You must always be aware of your surroundings. Help protect your spouse's space by warning them about this principle. Remember, it's all in the delivery. Say things like, “Babe I think you should give this a try, it won't hurt anything” or “Babe, I doubt that's a good idea, it can cause friction in a certain area” or “That person's energy is off, let's pray about this before we say yes”.

Trust me, I was big on the delivery from my wife. She may have said something that made sense, but if the delivery was bad, it was difficult to listen. I'm sure it worked the same way for her, so work on the delivery. It's not what you say but how you say it...

Chapter 8

Goal Setting

Importance Of Goal Setting

The New Man Principle #8: Short and Long -Term Goals

The plans of a diligent lead to profit as surely as haste leads to poverty. **(Proverbs 21:5)**

Goal setting is essential for transforming your life. One thing I learned from being in the streets is that we did not set real goals for our lives and families. We set goals that revolved around fashion or looking good, but they were not genuine plans. If I knew then what I know now, I would have had a long-term escape plan from the streets and the lifestyle long before I was forced out.

Most guys who hustle in the streets, if they are honest, will admit how much money they blew. If they had known better, they would have had a real vision or plan for their lives and families. Instead, they live day to day with no real direction, following whatever was popular at the moment.

Quick Story:

When I was released from prison, my main goal was to stay out of prison. Some may say that's not a real goal, but for me, it was significant because I wasn't good at staying out. I started setting short-term goals to support this overall goal. I needed to believe I could achieve it and disregard naysayers. Your goals are your goals, and your dreams are your dreams. Don't let anyone dictate what that means to you. Write them down or creative a vision board to make them visible and connect with those who can help you achieve your vision.

Habakkuk 2:2, talks about making the vision clear to those who see it and can run to it. Vision boards are important. It allows your loved ones to know what you're aiming for so they can be a part of that vision, helping you reach it. For those who can't see what you see, it's okay to separate yourself from them. Stop wasting time caring about what others think you should do. Generally, those who aren't doing much for themselves have the most to say about what you should do. Don't let it stop you from pursuing your dreams. Commit to prayer in all that you do and allow your plans to be established by God. (Proverbs 16:3).

How to Set Achievable Goals

Setting achievable goals requires a strategic approach. Here are some steps to help you set and achieve your goals:

1. **Define Your Goals Clearly:** Be specific about what you

want to achieve. Vague goals are difficult to measure and reach. For example, instead of saying, 'I would like to be healthier, set a specific goal like, I would like to lose ten pounds in three months.

2. **Set Smart Goals:** Ensure your goals are Specific, Measurable, Achievable, Relevant and Time-Bound. This framework helps you create clear and attainable goals.
3. **Break Down Your Goals:** Divide larger goals into smaller, manageable tasks. This makes them less overwhelming and easier to accomplish.
4. **Write Down Your Goals:** Documenting your goals helps solidify your commitment and provides a reference to track your progress.
5. **Create an Action Plan:** Outline the steps you need to take to achieve your goals, include deadlines and milestones to keep yourself accountable.
6. **Stay Flexible:** Be prepared to adjust your goals and plans as needed. Life is unpredictable, and being adaptable is key to staying on track.

NOTE TO SPOUSE:

Be supportive of your spouse's goals and dreams. They will appreciate you more. There is nothing like the one you love cheering you on and supporting your goals during your change process. This principle is important, and you will achieve your goals quicker with the support of each other.

Chapter 9

Finding Your Why

Quick Story:
Discovering My Why

Being in the streets, I lacked the true sense of purpose. My goals were superficial. I focused on short-term gains rather than long-term fulfillment. It wasn't until I took the time to reflect on my passions, strengths, and values that I began to uncover my true purpose. I realized that my experiences, both good and bad, had shaped me into someone who could inspire and guide others. My why became clear, to use my story and experiences to help others transform their lives and to find their purpose. The realization gave my life new meaning and direction.

Again, I am a natural leader and a helper. But for years I was wasting my role by leading the wrong arena. My gifts and talents were being prostituted by the streets and by people who didn't thrive in my role. I continued to fail because I was operating in the wrong environment. It was like wearing winter clothes in the summer. This is why you too might feel out of place. There is more to life and to your journey, you must dig deep and find your why. Once that's established, you're on your way to transforming your life and everything connected to you.

I now live and speak with conviction daily because I know what, when, and why I breathe. You will also by the end of this book. Again, just as I mentioned in chapter 3, one of my favorite Bible verses **Matthew 5:6,** Blessed are those who hunger and thirst for righteousness, for they shall be filled.

(As I continue to remind you) Reading this book, you are hungry and thirsty for transformation. God is getting ready to fill you up to the capacity of your hunger and thirst.

The Significance of Purpose

The New Man Principle #9:
Finding Your Why

Most people move through life without a clear purpose. They don't have a solid reason for doing what they do, which often leads to lack of direction and acceptance of failure. If you can't answer the question, why do you do what you do? With a meaningful purpose, then there's a problem. It's likely why you accept failure as an option. I used to think I was living to be successful because I wanted money and the American dream, but I realized that I was still empty inside, and that just was not enough. When you make money you're why, you end up doing anything to get it, typically with no integrity. Transformation requires a deeper WHY, a reason for what you do every single day. This deeper purpose will drive you towards your life's destination.

For me, it is no longer about money, success, or even family. Though, family is important in a major part of my connection. My why, the reason for my transformed life, is living out my purpose and understanding why the Lord allowed me to survive the things I've survived. It's the grace in my life that allowed me to endure.

Once you understand your why, life becomes easier. Decisions become easier, in every area of your life will align with your purpose. Clarity of vision equals acceleration toward the goal. Once your vision for your life is clear, achieving it becomes much easier and faster. My life now is easier to understand for anyone I come in contact with. Once your why is clear, no one can stop or deter you from it. It becomes the reason you live, the reason you breathe, and it will transform your life.

How To Discover Your Why

Discovering your why involves deep introspection to find your purpose and exploration. Here are some steps to help:

1. **Reflect on Your Passions:** Think about what activities make you feel most alive and fulfilled. What are you passionate about? What do you enjoy doing in your leisure time?

2. **Identify Your Strengths**: Consider your natural talent and skills. What are you good at? What do people often come to you for help with?

3. **Examine Values:** Reflect on your core values. What principles guide your decisions and actions? What is

most important to you in life?

4. **Look at Your Experiences:** Think about significant life experiences that have shaped you. What lessons have you learned? How have these experiences influenced your goals and desires?

5. **Ask Yourself Deep Questions:** Engage in deep self inquiry. Ask yourself questions like, "What impact do I want to have on the world? And what legacy do I want to leave behind?"

NOTE TO SPOUSE

You are a part of this journey with your significant other. It's essential to help each other discover why you've even existed. This won't take much arguing or fussing but prayer and fasting. Have daily conversations to bring out the best in each other, and work as a team to support one another. Find out what God wants you to do together. You are even closer than you think.

Chapter 10

Be Aware of The Rhythm of Life

Quick Story:
The Rhythm of Life (Romans 5:3-5)

Personally, I was in the rhythm of life. In and out of prison, coming home, starting over, and getting right back into that same lifestyle. It was a cycle I couldn't break. Yes, I made attempts to change and correct some things, but it wasn't until I decided to give God a full yes that I truly transformed my life. I stopped caring about what anyone else had to say or think about me and fully committed to change and transforming myself for good.

The difference this time was that I was making Godly decisions, not simply good decisions. Commitment to change was pivotal, and it can be for you as well if you follow these steps and embrace the journey ahead.

Understanding Life's Ups and Downs

The New Man Principle #10

The Rhythm of Life

The rhythm of life is the pattern that dictates the ups and downs we experience, including the repeated mistakes we continually make. It encompasses our daily routines, such as getting up, going to work, coming home, and repeating this cycle endlessly. The Rhythm of life can lead to frustration, especially when you don't understand your purpose or why you keep making the same mistake.

Understanding the rhythm of life is essential for transformation. Life will throw curveballs, and if you're not careful, it will dictate your direction. Embrace the journey, recognizing that transformation is a marathon, not a sprint. There will be ups and downs but staying motivated and celebrating small victories will keep you on track.

Steps to Embrace the Journey

1. **Acknowledge the Rhythm:** Recognize the patterns in your life and understand that difficulties are a natural part of the journey.
2. **Stay Motivated:** Find ways to stay motivated during challenging times. Surround yourself with positive influences and seek encouragement from others..
3. **Learn from Challenges:** Use challenges as opportunities for growth. Reflect on what you can learn

from each experience.

4. **Stay Positive:** Keep a positive mindset, even in the face of adversity. Trust that God is guiding you and that everything happens for a reason.

Practical Tips and Exercises

Exercise 1:

Daily Reflection: Spend a few minutes each day reflecting on your journey. Write down your thoughts and experiences.

Exercise 2:

Gratitude Practice: Keep a gratitude journal and write down things you're grateful for each day. Focus on the positive aspects of your journey.

Exercise 3:

Celebrate Achievements: Create a list of your achievements, both big and small. Celebrate each one and acknowledge your progress.

Exercise 4:

Seek Inspiration: Read books, listen to podcasts, or watch videos that inspire and motivate you. Surround yourself with positive influences.

Exercise 5:

Set Milestones: Set short-term and long-term milestones for your journey. Track your progress and adjust your goals as needed.

NOTE TO SPOUSE:

Support your spouse by embracing the journey together. Celebrate each other's achievements and stay motivated through challenges. Maintain a positive outlook and trust that God is guiding you both. Remember that transformation is a marathon, and your support is crucial in navigating the ups and downs. Try different things and explore each other's wants and needs.

Chapter 11

Reboot Regroup Reimagine

(Jeremiah 29:11)

Quick Story:

I was two years out of prison back in 2014 and found myself at a crossword. My life required a drastic change, and I knew I had to take some concrete steps to transform my future. I begin putting my plans on paper, imagining a life where I owned a house. I saw myself wearing suits and working in a corporate environment rather than being tied to the street.....

Although this vision wasn't my current reality, I believed in its possibilities. The next step was creating a vision board. I had never made one before and was just learning how to use email, I decided to give it a try. 30 years old, I got my first real job and started surrounding myself with working people. This new environment fueled my imagination and made my goals feel attainable. I worked on my credit and started telling people that I was going to buy a house. No one believed me, not even my wife at that time, but I stayed determined.

Eventually, my efforts paid off, and we were on our way to closing on our first home. This process taught me the power of faith and imagination. Every time I want to accomplish something new; I use this same process of reimagining my future. For example, I wanted to change my dress code from plain T-shirts and jeans to a more business casual look. Although I didn't own a suit, I envisioned myself wearing them. Not long after, a friend called me to church and gave me 20 to 30 brand-new suits that didn't fit him. Just like that, I had a new wardrobe that matched my reimagined self.

This experience confirmed that the process works. I encourage you to work the process of reimagining your life every chance you get. God knows what you need before you even ask. On this journey of transformation, you will need to reboot, regroup, and reimagine continually.

The New Man Principle #11
Regroup Reboot Reimagine

Sometimes in life you need to take a step back, breathe, rethink some things, and then go back at it full force. After understanding the rhythm of life and recognizing that life will throw curveballs, you must be ready to reboot, regroup, and reimagine before you start again just like you reboot a computer or phone. You also must reboot your life or journey to continue being successful. Recognize when something is off and take the necessary steps to recharge.

There will be times when you want to give up and reverting to your old ways, but it's not worth it. Take time to restart your engine. Vehicle requires regular service to last; you need regular rebooting to keep going strong, athletes take breaks during games to rest and recharge. You need to do the same to maintain effectiveness in your transformation journey. (I imagined myself wearing suits and I saw myself working in a corporate environment rather than being tied to the streets).

Building Resilience

Resilience is the ability to bounce back from adversity and continue moving forward. It's a crucial trait for handling life storms. Here are some ways to build resilience:

1. **Set Realistic Goals:** Break down the challenge into smaller, manageable goals. The problem seems less overwhelming and allows you to make steady progress.
2. **Develop a plan.** Create a detailed action plan outlining the steps you need to take to overcome the challenge. Having a clear plan provides direction and motivation.

Life's storms are inevitable, but how you handle them defines your journey. Resilience is the key to overcoming adversity and emerging stronger. Embrace challenges as opportunities for growth and stay committed to your vision.

Steps to Build Resilience

1. **Stay Positive:** Maintain a positive mindset, even in tough times. Focus on the lessons you can learn from each experience.
2. **Seek Support:** Surround yourself with supportive people who uplift and encourage you. Lean on your faith

and community for strength.

3. **Develop Coping Strategies:** Find healthy ways to cope with stress, such as prayer, meditation, exercise, or talking to a trusted friend or mentor.
4. **Stay Committed:** Stay committed to your goals and vision, even when faced with setbacks. Keep moving forward and don't give up.
5. **Celebrate Small Wins:** Celebrate each small victory along the way. These wins build momentum and remind you of your progress.

The Impact of Resilience

Resilience helps you navigate life's storms with grace and strength. It enables you to stay focused on your goals and maintain a positive outlook, even in challenging times. By building resilience, you can transform adversity into opportunities for growth and emerge stronger than ever.

Practical Tips and Exercises

Exercise 1:

Positive Affirmations: Create a list of positive affirmations and recite them daily. Focus on your strengths and capabilities.

Exercise 2:

Gratitude Practice: Keep a gratitude journal and write down things you're grateful for each day. Reflect on the positive aspects of your life.

Exercise 3:

Vision Board: Create a vision board with images and words that represent your goals and aspirations. Place it somewhere visible to remind you of your vision.

Exercise 4:

Seek Support: Identify supportive people in your life and reach out to them when you need encouragement. Build a strong support network.

Exercise 5:

Reflect on Challenges: Reflect on past challenges and how you overcame them. Identify the strengths and strategies you used and apply them to current challenges.

NOTE TO SPOUSE:

Support your spouse by being their pillar of strength during life's storms. Encourage them to stay positive and committed to their goals. Celebrate their victories and remind them of their resilience. Together, you can navigate any challenge and emerge stronger. Don't be afraid to rethink some things by rebooting, regrouping, and reimagining any situation WORKING THE PROCESS.

Chapter 12

The Power of Choices

Quick Story:
The Impact of a Single Choice

I have made many bad choices in life, too many to count, but one of the worst was when I decided to go back to selling drugs. It didn't start with drugs; it began with a simple choice to start drinking again after being free from hard liquor for about 3 1/2 years. I can remember like yesterday; it was the day my niece was killed by a car accident. That one moment led me back to old behaviors and ultimately back to prison. It was a hard lesson, but it made me realize that the choices you make today, dictate where you land tomorrow. The best choice I made was allowing the Lord to transform my life. Today, I am here to help others make better choices and transform their lives.

New Man Principle #12: The Power of Choices

Deuteronomy 30:19 says, "I have set before you life and death, blessing and cursing: therefore, choose life, that both thou and thy seed may live."

Every choice you make comes with challenges, especially good choices. I must continue to remind you that transformation is a marathon, not a sprint, and making consistent, good choices is key to success. You see, one bad choice can have a ripple effect changing your life for the worse. It will make you realize that the choices we make are important, big, or small. And sometimes not making a choice can be just as bad.

On this transformation journey, you will face life-changing choices for better or for worse. Each choice would dictate your destination at the end of the day. I've learned that it's the small foxes that destroy the vines. This means that even seemingly harmless, small choices can have significant consequences. Sin, for example, starts small but eventually leads to death. Meditate on some of the choices you've made, and I can assure you it's why you are where you are right now. REPEAT AFTER ME, "CHOICES."

Steps to Making Better Choices

1. **Consider the Consequences:** Before making a decision, think about the potential outcomes. How will this choice affect your future?
2. **Seek Wisdom:** Seek advice from trusted individuals and

pray for guidance. Proverbs 1:14 says, "Where no counsel is, the people fall: but in the multitude of counsellors there is safety."

3. **Stay Committed:** Stay committed to your good choices, even when faced with challenges. Perseverance is key to transformation.
4. **Learn from Mistakes:** When you make a bad choice, learn from it. Use it as a lesson to make better decisions in the future.
5. **Celebrate Progress:** Celebrate each good choice you make. Recognize the positive impact it has on your life.

The Impact of Choices

Every choice you make is important, whether good or bad. Good choices lead to positive outcomes and transformation, while bad choices can lead to setbacks and destruction. Understanding the power of choices and being intentional about your decisions can change the course of your life.

Practical Tips and Exercises

Exercise 1:

Decision Journal: Keep a journal where you document your decisions and their outcomes. Reflect on what you learn from each choice.

Exercise 2:

Pros and Cons List: Before deciding, create a list of pros and cons. Weigh the potential benefits and drawbacks.

Exercise 3:

Seek Guidance: Regularly seek guidance from mentors, friends, or family members. Discuss your choices and consider their input.

Exercise 4:

Reflect on Past Choices: Reflect on past decisions and their impact on your life. Identify patterns and areas for improvement.

Exercise 5:

Set Goals: Set clear goals for your life and make choices that align with those goals. Use your goals as a guide for decision-making.

NOTE TO SPOUSE:

Listen, I understand that you may have made some bad choices, but don't stay stuck there. Have a conversation about it and move forward. Don't hold on to the bad choices that were made last year, let alone ten years ago. That past hurt will continue to hurt today if you don't let go, and it's stopping you from growing. Today, call or text your spouse and say, "I forgive you for that bad choice you made years ago, and I pray that you can forgive me for the ones that I have made."

By doing this, you're not only forgiving each other but also making room for real transformation. Everything is a choice, including happiness. You have to wake up every single day and choose to be happy. Support your spouse in making better choices. I encourage open communication and discuss decisions together. Help each other weigh the pros and cons and seek wisdom from God and trusted individuals. Celebrate each other's progress and learn from mistakes together. Remember, transformation is a joint effort, and your support is crucial.

Chapter 13

Embracing the morning (Earl Riser)

The New Man Principle #13 (Rise Early)

Psalms 5:3 In the morning Lord you hear my voice, in the morning I lay my requests before You and wait expectantly.

I was in prison for about 11 1/2 years of my life, and during that time, we had to wake up early for breakfast, usually around 4 or 5:00 AM. Missing this meal was not an option. Depending on the dorm or prison, sleeping late could also put you at risk of danger. However, I was always an early riser. I'd be up before the lights came on, spinning that early time meditating and reading the word, preparing for the day. These habits I formed early in life. It's something about that early morning time in PRAYER!

No matter how late I stay up, I still manage to get up fairly early. But I'm also not up late unless it's an occasion., I'm writing this passage while everyone in my house is sleeping. I get up, pray, write, make breakfast, and get things prepared before everyone in the house wakes up. This allows me to get things done in peace. This practice is one of the many that will transform your life when dealing with time because there is not enough time in a day.

So, wake up early, prepare, and claim your day. This would allow you to be more organized and go into that day feeling accomplished. There have been times when I have been up late drinking and partying, yet I still force myself to wake up early. I spent many mornings meditating, reading and planning. This quiet time allowed me to set my intentions for the day and approach my task with clarity and purpose. Despite challenges, this routine calls for me to end up having productive days. This experience solidified my belief in the power of embracing the morning. No matter what I did the night before, getting up early is that much more important for me.

The days when I rise early are always more productive and fulfilling. For example, I remember when I was trying to get my business off the ground. Getting up early allowed me to have uninterrupted time to focus on my plans, strategies, and goals. I would spend the early hours researching, sending emails, and making phone calls before the rest of the world woke up. This head start gave me a competitive edge and significantly contributed to the success of my business. Rising early has numerous benefits that can transfer your life.

Benefits Of an Early Riser:

1. **Increase Productivity:** The quiet morning hours are perfect for focusing on important tasks without interruptions.

2. **Improve Mental Health and gives you time to spend in prayer:** Starting the day with a calm and clear mind reduces stress and anxiety.
3. **Better Physical Health**: Early risers often have more time for exercise, leading to improved physical health.
4. **Enhance Mood:** Morning routines can set a positive tone for the day, improving overall mood and outlook.
5. **Greater Organization:** Early morning provides an opportunity to plan and organize your day effectively.

NOTE TO SPOUSE:

You may not be an early riser, but don't give your spouse a hard time because they wake up early. Embrace it and understand the advantage it provides in getting things done. If you both adopt this principle, you can tackle chores and other tasks together or use that time for praying together. This is an important key to transforming your life and relationship.

Chapter 14

The Power Of Words

So much to be said about this principle, there is much evidence that proves this to be accurate:

I can remember always having negative self-talk about some of the things I saw in my wife, not understanding that the more I spoke about it, the harder it was to shift. Today, I understand the importance of words. Now, I'm cautious yet intentional about what I say about her and anything else in life.

Quick Story:

I was going through serious prayer and fasting as I approached my federal sentencing date. I was very positive about how things were going to go. I had been speaking positively the entire time, but I was asking God for a 5-year sentence, believing it was fair and just because of my behavior. Little did I know, I was speaking my outcome with conviction and belief.

Sure enough, the day came, and the judge was looking for

a reason to give me less time, but I believe I had canceled the possibility by my words, prayers, and belief. So, I received exactly what I asked for, 5 years on the dot. On the flip side, I should have been believing for less but limited by my belief based on my natural understanding, not considering that God was willing to honor my prayer and words at that moment. I tell you, speak life at all times because the heavens are listening.

Understanding The Impact of Words:

The New Man principle #14:
Understanding Your Words Has Power

Proverbs 18:21 "Death and Life are in the power of the tongue, and those who love it will eat its fruit."

This principle highlights the importance of words.

There is an old saying: your thoughts become your words, your words become your feelings, and your feelings become your actions, your actions become your habits, your habits become your lifestyle, and your lifestyle controls your destiny.

First and foremost, you must learn how to cast down certain thoughts before they come out of your mouth.

Matthew 6:31 "Take no thought saying"

Please do not speak every thought that comes into your mind. What happens is, is that you begin to shape your future with your thoughts, and your words allow them to manifest.

(2 Corinthians 10:5) Speaks about casting down evil imaginations or thoughts, which is important. If you do not do so, you will find yourself rebuilding these thoughts, and you shall have whatsoever you say.

(Psalms:45:1) States: My tongue is a pen of a ready writer. I paint pictures with my words, so, my question is, what are you saying today that's shifting your future or entering into it? Whichever one you focus on the most will win.

One of my favorite scriptures in the Bible is (**Mark 11:23)** Whosoever shall say unto this mountain, be thou removed, and be thou cast into the sea, and shall not doubt in his heart but shall believe that those things which he said shall come to pass, he should have whatever he says.

This scripture emphasizes that you must first start talking and believing what you say, and you should have it.

In the Court of Law, the word shall mean 100 percent happening without any doubt.

Some of us have been speaking death for so long, we wonder why things are not happening for us. Well, they are happening for you exactly as you say them. If I were you, I would go back and repent for some of those words you spoke. Start casting down, and reverse the word curses you've caused by the way you spoke. I don't care what it may look like in the natural "SPEAK LIFE."

Using Powerful and Empowering Language:

1. **Affirmations:** Incorporate positive affirmations into your daily routine, statements like I am capable, I am strong, I can achieve my goals, this can rewire your brain for

success.

2. **Encouragement:** Use words of encouragement with yourself and others. Make this a habit.
3. **Gratitude:** Expressing gratitude regularly can shift your focus from what's lacking to what's abundant. This positive outlook can transform your mindset.

Avoiding Negative Self-Talk

Negative self talk can be incredibly damaging. It can often lead to self-doubt in a defeatist attitude here are some strategies to combat it.

1. **Awareness:** Pay attention to your eternal dialogue. Recognize when you are engaging in negative self-talk.
2. **Challenge negative thoughts:** Questions of validity of negative thoughts. Replace them with positive or neutral statements.
3. **Refrain from negative situations:** Instead of focusing on what went wrong, look for what you can learn and how you can improve.

Benefits of mindful communication:

Mindful communication involves being present and intentional with your words. It fosters deeper connections and reduces misunderstandings. Here are some benefits.

1. **Improved relationships:** Communication builds trust and strengthens relationships.

2. **Reduce Conduct:** Being intentional with your words can prevent misunderstandings and reduce conflict.
3. **Greater Empathy:** Mindful communication encourages active listening and empathy, allowing for more meaningful interactions.

Positive Language Challenge:

Challenge yourself to replace negative words with positive ones for a week. Notice how this shift affects your mind set and interactions with others.

NOTE TO SPOUSE:

Be sure that you're not being moved by what you see or saw, rebuke those evil thoughts and words that you have been saying to and about your spouse. You shall have whatsoever you say, so today and forever more speak life about your spouse, kids and plans every single day over and over and over. Watch how you shape your future with your words!

(Matthew 12:36) everyone will have to give an account on judgement for every empty word they have spoken.

Chapter 15

Being Prepared

Quick Story:
The Power of Being Prepared

I was commissioned to go up to the Boston area for several months. Having lived in Florida all my life, I had never experienced the harsh northern winters. Knowing this, I had to prepare for the weather. I went shopping and over-prepared, ensuring I had more than enough warm clothing. The transition was difficult due to the cold, but I didn't panic because I was well-prepared. Had I gone unprepared, it would have been a very uncomfortable experience.

One particular day in Boston, the temperature dropped unexpectedly, and a severe snowstorm hit. Many of my colleagues were caught off guard, struggling to stay warm and safe. However, because I had prepared for the worst, I had all the necessary gear—thermal clothing, heavy boots, and a sturdy coat. While others scrambled to find solutions, I was able to carry on with my tasks, confident and comfortable. This experience reinforced the importance of preparation, not just for expected challenges but for the unexpected ones as well. Though it may seem small, it's critical.

Another significant instance of the power of preparation occurred during my transition from the streets to a more stable lifestyle. I realized that I needed to be ready for any setbacks and obstacles. I developed a detailed plan, setting aside savings, building a support network, and creating contingency plans for potential challenges. When setbacks did occur, I was able to navigate them smoothly, maintaining my progress and staying focused on my goals. This proactive approach was crucial in transforming my life and staying on track.

Importance of Preparation for Life's Challenges:

The New Man Principle #15:
You Can't Change the Weather, But You Can Be Prepared and Dressed for the Occasion

Understanding that storms will come is essential.

Psalms 34:19 states, "The righteous person may have many troubles, but the Lord delivers him from them all."

Another one of my favorite verses in the Bible is **James 1:2**, which reads, "Consider it pure joy, my brothers, and sisters, whenever you face trials of many kinds."

Notice it says "whenever" and not "if" —it's only a matter of time before the weather gets bad in your life. Prepare yourself by being watchful, communicating with the Lord, and being led by the Holy Spirit. This way, when the weather gets bad, you are prepared and discerning. This principle gives you a head start in understanding that when a storm comes, there is no need to panic.

You must adapt to circumstances beyond your control life is unpredictable, and sometimes, despite your best preparations, things can go wrong. Here are strategies to adapt when circumstances are beyond your control:

1. **Stay Flexible:** Be willing to adjust your plans as needed. Flexibility is crucial when dealing with unexpected changes.
2. **Maintain a Positive Attitude:** Focus on what you can control and maintain a positive outlook. This mindset will help you navigate challenges more effectively.
3. **Seek Support:** Don't hesitate to ask for help from friends, family, or professionals. Support networks are invaluable during tough times.
4. **Learn and Grow:** View challenges as opportunities to learn and grow. Each experience can teach you something valuable.

Strategies for Effective Preparation:

Effective preparation involves planning and forethought. Here are some strategies to help you prepare for life's challenges:

1. **Set Clear Goals:** Know what you want to achieve and create a plan to get there. Break your goals down into manageable steps.

2. **Create Contingency Plans:** Have backup plans for different scenarios. This ensures you are ready for the unexpected.

3. **Stay Informed:** Keep yourself informed about potential risks and challenges in your environment. Knowledge is power.

4. **Practice Regularly:** Regular practice and rehearsal can help you stay prepared. Whether it's a skill, a presentation, or an emergency drill, practice makes perfect.

Benefits of Being Prepared.
Being prepared offers numerous benefits:

1. **Peace of Mind:** Knowing you are ready for whatever comes your way provides peace of mind.

2. **Improved Outcomes:** Preparation increases the likelihood of positive outcomes, as you are better equipped to handle challenges.

3. **Greater Efficiency:** Being prepared allows you to use your time and resources more efficiently.

4. **Enhanced Reputation**: People respect and trust those who are well-prepared, which can enhance your personal and professional relationships.

Practical Steps and Exercises for Preparation

Exercise 1:
Goal Setting:

Write down your short-term and long-term goals. Break them into manageable steps and create a timeline for achieving them.

Exercise 2:
Contingency Planning:

Think about potential challenges you might face in different areas of your life (career, finances, health). Create contingency plans for each scenario.

Exercise 3:
Skill Practice:

Identify a skill you want to improve. Dedicate regular time to practice and refine this skill. Track your progress and adjust your practice routine as needed.

Exercise 4:
Emergency Preparedness:

Create an emergency plan for your household. Include important phone numbers, evacuation routes, and emergency supplies. Practice this plan with your family to ensure everyone knows what to do in case of an emergency.

NOTE TO SPOUSE:

Be sure that you're not the storm but the one helping your spouse prepare for the storm. When it comes, be an encourager, not a discourager. This transition is life-changing but not easy. Use prayer as your ultimate weapon during these times.

Chapter 16

The Pivot

Quick Story:
The Necessity of Shifting

I went through some challenging times while on the road to change. Staying connected with certain friends made it easier for me to go backward and indulge in old behaviors. These friends thought they were doing me a favor by reintroducing me to old avenues. This led me back to a lifestyle I worked so hard to shift from. I remember feeling frustrated and not understanding why I was caught up again. Through time and prayer, the Lord showed me my mistakes, revealing them in real-time, almost in slow motion. Not shifting was one of the main reasons I kept going backward. **Proverbs 26:11** says, "As a dog returns to its vomit, so fools repeat their folly".

The problem is that you might think you're strong enough, but you don't understand that while the spirit is willing, the flesh is weak. During this process, a complete shift is necessary. There are no exceptions to the rule regarding people, places, and things. If you have to question whether you should be somewhere or with someone, the answer is no.

The New Man Principle #16:
Don't Be Afraid to Pivot

Transforming your life involves learning to shift. This shift is crucial to your change process and can be a significant change. It includes changing the people, places, and things in your life. Yes, this means you will need to shift your company—old friends can't follow you on this journey. The places you used to frequent will no longer be suitable, and the things you used to do must be left behind.

Old people, old places, and old habits will keep you stagnant and hold you in place. Worse, they can trigger you to revert to old behaviors. Here's the kicker: even well-meaning friends who have your best interests at heart might inadvertently hinder your transformation because they only know one way to live. You must understand that, although you may love them, they can't go where you're going. If you don't master this shift, transformation will be difficult, if not impossible. You might think that some people are harmless or that stopping by certain places briefly is okay.

I assure you, it's not. You need to shift altogether for a season of your life to complete this transformation. Distractions can make it difficult to hear God's guidance, while other things are just outright detrimental.

Importance of Shifting

1. **Breaking Free from the Past:** Old habits and associations can keep you locked in a cycle of failure. To move forward, you need to break free.
2. **Avoiding Triggers:** Old environments and companions can trigger old behaviors.

   Eliminating these triggers is essential for lasting change.
3. **Creating New Patterns:** Shifting allows you to establish new, positive patterns and associations.
4. **Hearing God's Guidance:** Removing distractions helps you hear and follow God's guidance more clearly.

How to Shift

1. **Evaluate Your Circle:** Identify which relationships are supportive of your new path and which ones hold you back. Be honest with yourself about who can come along on your journey.
2. **Change Your Environment:** Avoid places that are tied to your old habits. Seek new, positive environments that support your growth.
3. **Develop New Habits:** Replace old habits with new, healthy ones. Engage in activities that promotes your new lifestyle.
4. **Seek Support:** Surround yourself with people who are on the same path or who support your transformation. Join groups or communities that align with your new

direction.

Benefits of Shifting

1. **Personal Growth:** You will grow and develop in ways you never thought possible.
2. **Enhanced Focus:** Removing distractions allows you to focus on your goals.
3. **Greater Resilience:** New, positive environments and relationships strengthen your ability to withstand challenges.
4. **Spiritual Clarity:** A clear mind and heart allow you to connect more deeply with God's plan for your life.

NOTE TO SPOUSE

As a spouse, offer your time and availability. What worked for me was spending weekends and nights with my wife and kids. We found activities to do together that helped me shift away from old people, places, and things. At this point, God will take the taste of some things out of your mouth but be his or her escape route. Support your spouse's journey by being an active participant in creating new, positive experiences together.

Chapter 17

There Is Safety in Counsel

Quick Story:
The Right Counsel at the Right Time

I had a promotion opportunity that was very profitable at my job, involving extensive travel. While the money was good, my frequent absences caused issues at home with my wife and kids. Seeking advice, I sat down with my spiritual father, Bishop Butts. He made it clear: "Son, you're out of position traveling and being away from your family too long. It's never about the money."

His words resonated with me. I realized that I had already spent enough time away from my family while in prison and that being away again was not the right choice. Conversely, a close friend advised me to take the promotion, arguing that such opportunities don't come every day and that my family would manage because I was bringing in money. While well-intentioned, his advice was not godly counsel. It sounded good because it aligned with what I wanted to do, but it wasn't the right decision for my family. The Bible says, "The blessing of the Lord makes rich and adds no sorrow to it," and this traveling was adding sorrow to my household.

The counsel you seek must align with the word and will of God. The will of God is His word, and His word is His will. By staying present and involved with my family, I was able to lead by example and avoid the mistakes of my past, such as being absent. A family man should be home, guiding his family.

The New Man Principle #17:
There Is Safety in Counsel

Seeking counsel is a critical aspect of transforming your life. **Proverbs 11:14** states, "In the multitude of counsel there is safety." This principle emphasizes the importance of seeking guidance to gain a godly advantage in your transformation journey. However, it is essential to be strategic about whom you seek counsel from. Not everyone is equipped to offer the guidance you need. God will send you people who can unlock your destiny if you seek them.

Jeremiah 3:15 says,"Then I will give you shepherds after my own heart, who will lead you with knowledge and understanding."

To be successful in your transformation, you must be receptive to this counsel.

For example, if you are a married man or woman, it is beneficial to surround yourself with married friends. While there are exceptions, typically, those who share your life circumstances can give more relevant advice. Single individuals often think and give advice from a single person's perspective. However, godly single people can offer valuable wisdom and help you make sound decisions. Be very intentional in seeking this counsel.

Importance of Seeking Godly Counsel

1. **Guidance and Wisdom:** Godly counsel provides the guidance and wisdom you need to navigate life's challenges.
2. **Alignment with God's Will**: It ensures that your decisions align with God's will and word.
3. **Support and Encouragement:** Having a support system of godly individuals offers encouragement and strength during tough times.
4. **Avoiding Pitfalls:** It helps you avoid the pitfalls of well-meaning but ungodly advice.

How to Seek Counsel

1. **Be Selective:** Seek counsel from godly leaders or individuals who have demonstrated wisdom and integrity.
2. **Pray for Guidance**: Ask God to lead you to the right people who can provide the counsel you need.
3. **Be Receptive:** Be open to receiving advice and correction, even if it is not what you want to hear.
4. **Verify with Scripture:** Ensure that the counsel you

receive aligns with biblical principles.

Benefits of Seeking Counsel

1. **Safety and Security:** Seeking counsel provides a sense of safety and security in your decisions.
2. **Growth and Development:** It promotes personal growth and spiritual development.
3. **Clarity and Direction:** Counsel helps you gain clarity and direction for your life's path.
4. **Strength and Resilience:** It builds strength and resilience to face challenges.

NOTE TO SPOUSE

Always seek godly counsel. Ask yourself what does the word says about your situation and seek advice from godly individuals. Avoid relying solely on friends' opinions. Not all good advice is God advice. By seeking godly counsel, you can filter out potential nonsense and ensure that your decisions are aligned with God's will.

Chapter 18

Do Not Put Much Confidence in Your Flesh

Quick Story:
The Consequences of Fleshly Decisions

IN my backslide, I made desperate decisions due to financial losses. These decisions were driven by the flesh, leading me to pick up old habits I had previously overcome. Had I remained spiritually grounded, I would have been patient and sought guidance for my next move. Instead, my desperation led to disobedience and regression.

Now, for those who don't understand being led by the spirit, by this point in the book, you should know that being spiritually sound is the only way to truly transform. You are going to have to get into your word and get to the altar to figure this one out because it sounds spooky if you don't already do this every single day. In a nutshell, you will have to spend time with the Father and be intentional about spending time with Him. Set an alarm clock or a reminder, whatever you have to do to make sure you're in your word and spending time with God. That way, your flesh won't be in charge.

The New Man Principle #18:
Do Not Put Too Much Confidence in Your Flesh

Galatians 5:16-26 urges us to "walk in the Spirit" so we do not fulfill the desires of the flesh. I don't want to sound spooky or over the top with this principle, but some things aren't going to change without spiritual help and guidance. Early on, I talked about having that anchor, which is that higher power, and that higher power is having a spiritual relationship with Christ. The Holy Spirit will lead and guide you on this transformation journey.

The problem is that we tend to rely on the flesh, and the flesh will let you down every single time. Jesus famously said, "The spirit is willing, but the flesh is weak." Enough said right there. We can end this chapter on that quote alone, but I have to give you a little more so you will be able to make sense out of this principle.

You see, the flesh and the spirit will constantly be at war, and it depends on which one you feed the most as to who will win this battle. The crazy part about this concept is that neither is ever satisfied. The more you feed your spirit, the hungrier your spirit becomes. The more you feed your flesh, the hungrier your flesh becomes. Either way, they both have expandable appetites.

Proverbs 27:20 says, "Hell and destruction are never full; so the eyes of man are never satisfied." You must keep in mind that the flesh wants what it wants and when it wants it. That alone will not only get you in trouble but will set you back in your transformation process. **Romans 7,** gives an interesting concept on the battle of flesh and spirit. It states that even when you want to do right, evil is always there. With that evil being present, you have to be spiritually minded to pull this off because you will never be exempt from temptation.

This is an everyday battle that you have to constantly be aware of. There are three things that stands out the most involving temptation:

1. **Power:** You will be tempted to have power in certain areas, and how you approach this power will be important for your success or failure.

2. **Money:** Money will also test your flesh's limits as well as how you respond to having it or not having it. Having a lot of it in your flesh could destroy you. Having none of it your flesh could breed desperation. Be careful how you respond either way. Just know for certain that desperation leads to disobedience.

3. **Lust of the flesh:** This part of the flesh needs to be tamed at all times. This equals pleasures, so not just physical sex but also anything that is considered a pleasure. You must be spiritually minded when approaching these temptations. In a nutshell, without spirituality, your flesh will control your decisions, which will make transformation impossible. Yes, you can make minor or temporary changes, but transformation will be impossible being led by your flesh.

Steps to Walking in the Spirit

1. **Pray Daily:** Spend time in prayer daily, seeking guidance and strength from the Holy Spirit.
2. **Read the Word:** Study the Bible regularly to understand God's will and strengthen your spirit.
3. **Meditate on God's Word:** Meditate on Scripture and let it guide your thoughts and actions.
4. **Seek Accountability:** Find an accountability partner who can support you in your spiritual walk.
5. **Stay Connected to the Church**: Stay connected to a church community for support and encouragement.

The Impact of Walking in the Spirit

Walking in the Spirit helps you avoid the pitfalls of the flesh and stay on the path of transformation. It enables you to make decisions that honor God and lead to lasting change. By relying on the Holy Spirit, you can overcome temptations and live a life that reflects God's will.

NOTE TO SPOUSE

Help your mate with this principle by maintaining a continuous prayer life. Even when they slip, be there to encourage them and pray with them and also pray for them because the flesh is a tough opponent to battle with.

Chapter 19

Get to Know Yourself

Quick Story:
Discovering My True Self

This goes hand in hand with what I said earlier about taking inventory.

While I was incarcerated, I found myself reading all the hood novels that were being passed around. I would finish a book in one night—I was a reader by nature. As I began to discover myself, I realized that I was a reader, but I was reading the wrong material. Let me say this: there's nothing wrong with reading hood books or urban stories, but for me, it was the wrong material. I was wasting time reading about the life I was trying to get away from. I was reading it because it was popular, not because I actually liked it.

I was always different from others, but I didn't know why. Once I discovered who I was, I was able to embrace my uniqueness and stand out by being myself. Knowing your triggers and what drives you is crucial. For example, being able to provide for my family drives me. When I can't, it triggers me. But knowing this, I make sure to prepare for tough times so that my household remains stable.

Dig deep, meditate, know who you are, and transform into the best version of yourself without caring about what others think. If you know me, you know that I'll be myself around whoever, regardless of their opinions.

The New Man Principle #19:
Get to Know Yourself—Your Triggers and What Drives You

Psalm 139:23-24 reads, "Search me, O God, and know my heart; try me and know my thoughts; and see if there be any grievous way in me and lead me in the way everlasting!"

Most men struggle with identity due to a lack of parental guidance or the influence of their environment. Although other factors also play a role, these two are foundational. Identity is a key factor in transforming your life. You must know who you are and whose you are to become what you should be. You have to study yourself and spend time getting to know yourself.

It's funny how we can live a certain way for so long but not truly enjoy life because we are not comfortable in our skin. We are so quick to conform to the world that we forget to be ourselves. We should be more concerned with what's acceptable to God **(Romans 12:2).** Most of the time, we are the way we are because of where we came from. However, if you are intentional about studying yourself, you will discover who you really are.

Once you know yourself, you will know what you like and

dislike, enabling you to make necessary changes. The reason I mention parental guidance is that most of our learned behavior comes from our parents and what we were taught. Our environment shapes us based on who we are surrounded by, but that doesn't necessarily mean we are walking in our true selves. By getting to know yourself, you will discover who you really are through meditation and the Word of God.

Importance of Self-Discovery

1. **Understanding Triggers:** Knowing what triggers, you help you overcome negative reactions.
2. **Identifying Motivators:** Understanding what drives you helps you focus on your goals.
3. **Embracing Authenticity:** Discovering your true self allows you to live authentically and confidently.
4. **Personal Growth:** Self-discovery is essential for personal growth and transformation.

How to Get to Know Yourself

1. **Meditate:** Spend time in quiet reflection to understand your thoughts and feelings.
2. **Study the Word:** Use the Bible as a guide to discover your true identity in Christ.
3. **Reflect on Your Past:** Look at your past experiences to understand your behaviors and patterns.
4. **Journal:** Write down your thoughts and feelings to gain

insight into your triggers and motivator.

Benefits of Self-Discovery

1. **Improved Relationships:** Knowing yourself helps you build better relationships with others.
2. **Enhanced Decision-Making:** Understanding your triggers and motivators leads to better decision-making.
3. **Increased Confidence:** Being comfortable in your own skin boosts your confidence.
4. **Greater Resilience:** Knowing yourself helps you bounce back from setbacks more easily.

The Impact of Knowing Yourself

Knowing yourself allows you to make informed decisions and align your actions with your true identity. It helps you avoid negative influences and stay focused on your transformation. By understanding your triggers and motivations, you can develop strategies to overcome challenges and grow in your journey.

Practical Tips and Exercises

Exercise 1:

Daily Journaling: Set aside time each day to journal about your thoughts, feelings, and experiences. Reflect on what you learn about yourself.

Exercise 2:

Self-Reflection Questions: Ask yourself questions like, "What did I do well today?" "What could I have done better?", and "What did I learn from this experience?"

Exercise 3:

Seek Feedback: Repeatedly ask for feedback from trusted individuals. Use their insights to inform your self-discovery.

NOTE TO SPOUSE

Understand the triggers of your spouse by also studying him or her. Study yourself and share your weaknesses and strengths with each other. Don't use them as weapons against each other. Help each other overcome challenges and support each other's transformation. Remember, transformation is ongoing.

Chapter 20

Check Your Pride at the Door

Quick Story:
The Dangers of Pride

I shared a story earlier that rocked my business world. My old employer reached out to me to have a conversation, but I was being prideful due to the way our relationship ended. My pride stopped me from having that conversation. Moreover, when I was struggling spiritually, my church family was reaching out to me, but I would rather not let anyone know that I was failing.

This was an example of pride. My wife didn't have a chance of knowing my struggles at the time. For one, she was more like the "I told you so" type back then, so she had no shot at hearing my issues. Yes, we should have had a better relationship at that time, but again, pride was an issue, and it played a major role in my relapsing and back sliding.

Pride made me feel exempt from certain things, but the truth is that it's only the grace of God that can keep you from those things. Basically, pride makes you feel untouchable. Check pride by recognizing it and humbling yourself with understanding. This will be your greatest capture. It is in a man's nature to be prideful. Pride breeds all types of negativities, and most of all, it breeds dishonesty. When pride is involved, the truth may be embarrassing, you will tell a lie in a minute because of pride. So be certain not to allow pride to stand in the way of your transformation.

The New Man Principle #20: Check Your Pride at the Door

Proverbs 16:18 says, "Pride goes before destruction, a haughty spirit before a fall." Listen, we've all been there, some more than others, but I'll tell you now, if transformation is the goal, pride needs to be eliminated from the picture. The problem with pride is that it blinds reasoning. Pride stands in the way of decisions, it causes you to miss out on blessings, and, more importantly, brings you to a fall. Pride will even stand in the way of common sense. I can sit back and measure a situation and immediately sense pride based on the information that's given.

Isaiah 14:12-14 shows how Lucifer was defeated by pride. When I think of pride, I think of Satan and his angels who allowed pride to be their downfall. When I think of pride, I think of Pharaoh in Exodus, who had multiple chances to do right but refused to put pride aside, leading to his own destruction.

The Dangers of Pride

1. **Blinds Reasoning:** Pride makes it difficult to see things clearly and make rational decisions.

2. **Hinders Blessings:** Pride can cause you to miss out on opportunities and blessings because you refuse to humble yourself.
3. **Leads to Destruction:** Ultimately, pride leads to a fall and can destroy your progress.
4. **Prevents Honest Reflection:** Pride makes it difficult to admit mistakes and learn from them.

How to Overcome Pride

1. **Recognize Pride:** The first step is acknowledging that pride is an issue.
2. **Seek Humility:** Actively work on being humble. Understand that humility is not thinking less of yourself but thinking of yourself less.
3. **Ask for Help:** Don't be afraid to seek help from others, whether it's friends, family, or mentors. They can provide a perspective that you might be missing.
4. **Stay Grounded in Faith:** Let your spiritual beliefs guide you. Regular prayer and reflection can help keep pride in check.

Benefits of Overcoming Pride

1. **Improved Relationships:** Humility allows you to connect with others on a deeper level.
2. **Greater Opportunities:** When you're humble, you're more open to learning and growth, which leads to new

opportunities.

3. **Personal Growth:** Overcoming pride is essential for personal development and transformation.
4. **Spiritual Growth:** Humility is a key component of spiritual maturity and growth.

NOTE TO SPOUSE

Pride will have to be removed strategically. No one really wants to admit that pride is a problem, but as a discerning spouse, you must recognize this spirit and address it with a plan. Remember, as a spouse, you have influence, but it's all in how you use it. You will be the number one reason why your spouse transforms. Trust the process and ensure that you're not being prideful either.

Chapter 21

Celebrate small victories

The New Man Principle #21: Celebrate Small Victories

Quick Story:
The Impact of Celebrating Every Achievement

On this road to transformation, every time I made an accomplishment, I looked for a reason to go out with my family to celebrate. Each celebration made me feel like a giant, ready to crush the next goal or even stand toe to toe with a lion. When I got my first job at the age of 30, I celebrated like I had just won the lottery. When I got my GED, I celebrated like I had graduated from high school. When my credit score went up five points, I celebrated it. I used to curse many years ago, and before I stopped completely, I would celebrate myself every day I went without cursing. It's been years now.

The more I celebrated these victories, the more strength and motivation I gained to push harder. Although this may seem simple, try it, and see. Even your kids don't understand how small these victories might seem. All they know is that Daddy did something great. At this point, you'll start feeling like a hero, and for a man, this feeling is essential. You are a hero—you just don't know it yet.

The New Man Principle #21: Celebrate Small Victories

Luke 15:7 says, "I say unto you, that likewise joy shall be in heaven over one sinner that repenteth, more than over ninety and nine just persons, which need no repentance.

This principle is as important as any other principle. On your transformation journey, there will be days when you want to give up, and days when you would like to go backward. However, there will also be small accomplishments. These may seem insignificant to some people, but for you, they are momentum shifters. Every accomplishment, big or small, is significant. Here's why: every time you accomplish something new; it gives you ambition for the next goal.

Never let anyone tell you what should be celebrated and never let anyone dictate the size of your victory. If you understand this principle, it will drive you to pursue victories. It gives you a reason to chase something good. Again, Jesus states in **Luke 15** that joy should be in heaven over one sinner who repents is greater than over ninety-nine just people who need no repentance. He is saying that heaven celebrates what might seem small to us but is great to heaven. The same thing applies to you—when you gain momentum, celebrate it.

This celebration should be enjoyed with your family or loved ones. Whether it's a graduation, a good grade, passing an exam, getting a new job or promotion, or any other victory, be sure to celebrate it. After the celebration, move forward and look for the next victory moment.

Importance of Celebrating Small Victories

1. **Building Momentum:** Celebrating small victories gives you the motivation to pursue bigger goals.
2. **Positive Reinforcement:** It reinforces positive behavior and achievements, encouraging you to continue.
3. **Boosting Morale:** Celebrations boost your morale and make you feel accomplished.
4. **Strengthening Relationships:** Celebrating with loved ones strengthens your relationships and creates lasting memories.

How to Celebrate Small Victories

1. **Acknowledge Achievements:** Recognize and acknowledge every achievement, no matter how small.
2. **Share with Loved Ones:** Celebrate with family and friends who support your journey.
3. **Set Milestones:** Break down your goals into smaller milestones and celebrate each one.
4. **Reward Yourself:** Give yourself a treat or reward for your hard work and dedication.

Benefits of Celebrating Small Victories

1. **Increased Motivation:** Celebrations keep you motivated and focused on your goals.
2. **Improved Self-Esteem:** Recognizing your achievements boosts your confidence and self-esteem.
3. **Enhanced Resilience:** Celebrating small victories helps you stay resilient during challenging times.
4. **Positive Outlook:** It fosters a positive outlook on life and your transformation journey.

NOTE TO SPOUSE

Join your spouse in celebrating their victories. Acknowledge their achievements and celebrate together. Your support and encouragement are crucial in maintaining motivation and momentum. Together, you can enjoy the journey and celebrate each step towards transformation.

Chapter 22

Use Prayer as a Weapon

(Luke 18:1)

Quick Story:
The Power of Prayer in Dangerous Situations:

I can remember running the streets at a high level, but because I knew how to pray, I was always protected from some of the most dangerous situations ever. There are things I walked away from that only prayer could have shielded me from. From dodging bullets to making it through multiple prison sentences with favor, prayer has been my shield. It protects you from unseen dangers and grants you uncommon favor. Take this simple principle seriously, and it will take you to the promised land, getting you farther than any other principle I can name.

The new Man Principle #22: Use Prayer as a Weapon

A man ought always to pray and not faint. **Luke 18:1** Prayer is important—it's your everything at the end of the day. It's what you need to transform. Be advised that transformation cannot take place without prayer. In **Ephesians 6**, Paul gives household instructions, and then he offers final advice: "Finally, be strong in the Lord and in his mighty power." He goes on to discuss the real battle of life, which is not a battle of flesh and blood but a spiritual battle. Without prayer, there is no way to fight this battle at all.

Therefore, I urge you if you're going to transform, you will need a prayer life, 100%. There are unseen battles that you cannot fight without prayer. Prayer is a real weapon, stronger than any gun, you can ever carry and bigger than any rocket launcher the army ever made. Prayer is not a wish list to God—He knows what you need. It is simple communication between you and God that grants Him permission to interfere with your daily life.

Steps to Developing a Strong Prayer Life

1. **Pray Daily:** Make prayer a daily habit. Set aside specific times each day to connect with God.
2. **Be Specific:** Be specific in your prayers. Tell God your needs, desires, and concerns. Trust that He hears and answers.
3. **Listen:** Spend time listening to God during prayer. Be

open to His guidance and direction.

4. **Pray with Others:** Pray with your spouse, family, or friends. There is strength in collective prayer.
5. **Stay Persistent:** Be persistent in your prayers. Don't give up, even when you don't see immediate results.

The Impact of Prayer

Prayer is a powerful weapon that provides guidance, protection, and strength. It connects you with God and allows Him to work in your life. By developing a strong prayer life, you can navigate life's challenges with divine support and achieve lasting transformation.

Prayer Journal: Keep a prayer journal where you document your prayers, God's answers, and your reflections.

IN THE WORDS OF MY FEARLESS LEADER OVERSEER PROPHETESS WILMA BUTTS, "MUCH PRAYER, NO POWER. LITTLE PRAYER, LITTLE POWER. NO PRAYER, NO POWER."

NOTE TO SPOUSE

Support your spouse in developing a strong prayer life. Pray together and encourage each other to stay persistent in prayer. Your collective prayers can strengthen your relationship and provide divine support for your transformation journey.

Chapter 23

Always Have a Positive Approach

Quick Story:

A long time ago, during one of my prison stints, I started to notice how most people with high blood pressure all had anger problems. They would get all worked up and angry, causing their blood pressure to rise. So, I said to myself, since anger is probably inevitable, I will only allow myself 30 seconds to be angry, then I will snap out of it. That way, I could stay healthy. That was back in 1999, and until this day, I live by that same rule. Whenever I see myself getting angry, I let it take place for only a few seconds or a few minutes, then boom, I snap out of it. I understand what anger can do to affect a man.

Get anger out of your system by understanding its negative effects and the impact it has on your decisions.

The New Man Principle #23:
Always Have a Positive Approach—Anger is Not You; It's a

Trick of the Enemy

James 1:19-20 says, "Human anger does not produce the righteousness that God desires". **Ecclesiastes 7:9** states, "Do not be quickly provoked in your spirit, for anger resides in the lap of a fool."

On the road to transformation, there will be moments of anger and frustration because you're trying to break habits and shift from the known to the unknown. It would be a disservice for me to say there wouldn't be times when anger will set in. The key is recognizing it before it consumes you.

Whenever anger sets in, it breeds disobedience and bad decisions. It's impossible to make logical decisions when angry. In fact, some of the worst decisions known to man are made when a man gets angry. He can no longer make rational decisions and is only capable of moving based on emotions, which usually doesn't end well.

So, staying positive is key to transforming, regardless of what things may look like. This will take practice—lots of practice—because it's in human nature for a man to get angry. Don't be surprised if anger creeps up. Just understand that anger is temporary, and you must get past it as soon as possible.

Steps to Managing Anger and Frustration

1. **Recognize Anger:** Acknowledge when you feel anger. Understanding the triggers helps you manage your emotions.

2. **Take a Pause:** Take a moment to pause and breathe before reacting. This helps you respond calmly and rationally.
3. **Practice Self-Control:** Develop self-control to manage your reactions. Avoid impulsive actions driven by anger.
4. **Seek Solutions:** Focus on finding solutions to the issues causing your frustration. Stay proactive and positive.
5. **Pray for Peace:** Ask God for peace and patience. Trust that He will help you manage your emotions and stay positive.

The Impact of a Positive Approach

Maintaining a positive approach helps you navigate challenges with grace and resilience. It prevents anger and frustration from taking control and leading to negative outcomes. By staying positive, you can make better decisions and stay focused on your transformation journey.

Practical Tips and Exercises

Exercise 1:

Daily Reflection: Reflect on your emotions each day. Identify triggers and think about how you can manage them better.

Exercise 2:

Breathing Exercises: Practice deep breathing exercises to calm yourself when feeling angry or frustrated.

Exercise 3:

Positive Affirmations: Create a list of positive affirmations and recite them daily. Focus on staying positive and calm.

NOTE TO SPOUSE

Support your spouse in managing anger. Encourage open communication and help each other stay positive. Be a source of peace and comfort and work together to find solutions to challenges. Your support is crucial in maintaining a positive approach and fostering transformation.

Chapter 24

You Can't Afford to Be Frustrated

(Ephesians 4:26)

Quick Story:
The Consequences of Frustration

When I was dealing with business failure, it caused me to be frustrated. That frustration was the start of a series of bad decisions. I didn't understand why everything was going wrong. It seemed as if everything I tried to do failed. Even at home, it became a war zone as a result of my frustration. I was angry, frustrated, and confused all at the same time. I literally gave up on everything. Furthermore, I shut down the business and didn't want to be bothered. Even at home, my wife had become my enemy. We couldn't see eye to eye on anything, and our marriage was in trouble. The frustration didn't allow me to think logically, and before I knew it, I had a "don't give a dang mentality."

All of this was a result of frustration. It cost me my freedom and almost cost me my family. By the grace of God, I was able to reunite with my family. However, you reading this book may not get that opportunity—I don't know. But what I do know is that you cannot afford to be frustrated. The moment you feel it, you must pray, seek counseling or help, and address that feeling at once.

The New Man Principle #24: You Can't Afford to Be Frustrated

Some people may think anger and frustration are the same, but they're not. Anger is an emotion, while frustration comes when things are not favorable. During this time of transformation, there will be moments when frustration will set in. But I tell you that you can't afford to go there. Some things will make you angry on the surface but getting frustrated breeds a flurry of bad decisions. Allowing yourself to get frustrated is a recipe for setbacks, and setbacks are detrimental to this process. Frustration will cause you to give up. I treat frustration the same way I treat anger.

The Dangers of Frustration

1. **Bad Decisions:** Frustration clouds judgment, leading to poor choices.
2. **Setbacks:** Frustration often results in setbacks that can derail your progress.
3. **Relationship Strain**: It can cause conflicts and misunderstandings in relationships.
4. **Mental Health:** Prolonged frustration can negatively impact your mental health.

How to Manage Frustration

1. **Recognize the Signs:** Be aware of the signs of frustration and address them early.
2. **Pray and Seek Guidance:** Use prayer and seek guidance to help manage your emotions.
3. **Stay Positive:** Focus on positive aspects and solutions rather than problems.
4. **Take Breaks:** When frustration sets in, take a break to clear your mind and regain focus.

Benefits of Managing Frustration

1. **Better Decision-Making:** Clear thinking leads to better decisions.
2. **Progress:** Managing frustration helps you stay on track with your goals.
3. **Healthy Relationships:** It fosters healthier and more supportive relationships.
4. **Mental Well-Being:** Reducing frustration improves your overall mental health.

The Impact of Overcoming Frustration

Overcoming frustration helps you stay focused and motivated on your transformation journey. It prevents setbacks and bad decisions, allowing you to make better choices and stay on track. By managing frustration, you can navigate challenges with grace and resilience.

Practical Tips and Exercises

Exercise 1:

Daily Reflection: Reflect on your emotions each day. Identify triggers and think about how you can manage them better.

Exercise 2:

Positive Affirmations: Create a list of positive affirmations and recite them daily. Focus on staying positive and calm.

Exercise 3:

Seek Help: Talk to a trusted friend, mentor, or counselor about your frustrations. Seek their support and guidance.

NOTE TO SPOUSE

A lot of these notes may seem repetitive, and they are by design. If you hear it enough, you just might take action. However, your spouse needs you to listen and encourage them. Transformation is not for the faint of heart—it's a grind and a marathon, not a sprint. So, it will behoove you as a spouse to be there unconditionally, believing in him or her, and being their biggest cheerleader. When you sense frustration, take immediate action. Do not hesitate.

Chapter 25

Spend Time with Those you Love and Care For

The New Man Principle #25
The Power of Family Time

Before going to prison this last time, I had started to spend more time with family, and it kept me safe; it kept me out of the way. But when I got frustrated and started making bad decisions, I was no longer available for my family. When I got arrested, all I thought about was my family and the peace of mind that I got from being around them. So, when I was released, I embraced this principle, and all my plans are now based around my family and loved ones. My business includes my wife and kids, along with everything I do. Everything I need is in the house.

The New Man Principle #25:
Spend Time with Those You Love and Care For—They Need the New You

Ecclesiastes 9:9 talks about enjoying life with the wife whom you love. I see this as not only referring to your wife, but your loved ones as a whole. This principle gives you an automatic advantage to stand out from the streets or away from the outside world.

This principle will hide you from the world; it becomes your peace and your new normal. Your kids will start getting used to you being there, and it allows you to be in a position to pour into them the way you should.

By faith my wife and I are strategic about spending time with each other and the kids. Date night, vacations, bible study and family meetings. Don't let the world teach your kids you are the teacher in your own home. When was the last time you spent the entire weekend with family ONLY?

Be sure to turn down events occasionally if you have family plans, no matter what others may think it's about the family God allowed you to create.

The Importance of Spending Time with Loved Ones:

1. **Strengthening Bonds:** Spending time with loved ones strengthens your relationships and creates lasting memories.
2. **Emotional Support:** Your presence provides emotional support and stability to your family.
3. **Positive Influence:** Being around your loved ones allows you to be a positive influence in their lives.
4. **Peace and Stability:** It creates a peaceful and stable

environment, which is crucial for personal transformation.

How to Spend Quality Time with Loved Ones:

1. **Prioritize Family Time**: Make family time a priority in your daily schedule.
2. **Engage in Activities Together:** Find activities that everyone enjoys and engage in them together.
3. **Be Present:** When you are with your loved ones, be fully present. Put away distractions like phones and work.
4. **Communicate Openly:** Encourage open and honest communication with your family members.

Benefits of Spending Time with Loved Ones:

1. **Improved Mental Health:** Spending time with loved ones reduces stress and improves mental health.
2. **Stronger Family Unit:** It strengthens the family unit and builds a support system.
3. **Increased Happiness:** Being around loved ones increases happiness and life satisfaction.
4. **Better Parenting:** It allows you to be a better parent by being involved in your children lives.

NOTE TO SPOUSE:

Help with this principle by making things comfortable for your spouse to be in your presence all the time. Sacrifice for the things he or she likes, and don't be selfish. This is a significant yet sensitive principle, but it is needed. Most importantly, give each other the grace to make mistakes. Remember, the kids need you both and need to see you both giving sound advice and spending quality time together.

Chapter 26

Identity—The Real Fight is Spiritual

C**Olossians3:10** and have put on the new man, which is renewed in the knowledge after the image of him that created him.

You see, the trick is to keep you away from Christ so you will NEVER discover your true identity. Most of us are shaped by our environment and the enemy doesn't want you to know the truth and the only way to do so is with a relationship with the one who created you.

Quick Story:
Discovering My Own Identity

I take myself as an example. Again, I grew up in a household where my mom and dad had been together most of my life, and my mom did all the cooking. It was traditional in my household for my mom to cook day in and day out, no matter what. However, as I transformed into my own, I discovered that I enjoy cooking. My uncles on my mom's side and my brothers were all good at cooking, even my grandfather, was a good cook. Although cooking was my mom's job in my dad's household, it's not how I run my house.

Like I mentioned early on My wife cooks sporadically, and she can cook, but I also enjoy cooking. It's part of who I am, but I had to discover this within myself. Otherwise, I would have forced my wife to do all the cooking. Now, I believe I cook more than her, and I enjoy it. Just because my dad didn't cook, and my mom did all the cooking doesn't mean that that should be my way of life. Be who you are, not who you learned to be.

The New Man Principle #26:
Identity—The Real Fight is Spiritual

I cannot stress this enough. The enemy doesn't want you to become who you should be. **John 17:16** says, "They are not of the world, even as I am not of the world." Identity is crucial for transformation. It goes hand in hand with evaluating yourself and searching for whom you really are. We spend so much time being who we see in others that we often don't know who we are.

You are not a born murderer, a drug dealer, or any other negative identity you may have adopted. These are all results of learned behavior and familiar spirits. Dig deeper and start studying yourself to see what you like or dislike. It's time to take off that mask you've been wearing and be who you are called to be.

Factors Affecting Your Identity

1. **Environment:** Your surroundings, including your

neighborhood and parents, shape and affect you. You pick up many traits from your environment, whether good or bad.

2. **Credible People:** These are the people you deem credible and mimic, whether they are right or wrong. You must discover yourself beyond their influence.

3. **Repetitious Information:** If you hear something repeatedly, you start believing it and adopting its ways. Be careful not to become what you've seen and heard without examining if it's truly you.

4. **Experiences:** What you go through, whether good or bad, shapes who you become. However, this doesn't mean this is who you are.

Examine yourself to find the real you.....

Discovering Your True Self

It's important to take time to study yourself and understand who you truly are. This involves spending time in self-reflection, meditation, and seeking guidance from the Word of God. You must strip away the layers of learned behaviors and influences to uncover your true identity.

NOTE TO SPOUSE:

Help each other discover who you truly are. Your identity is important. It's good to try new things, but don't base your partnership on others. You are fearfully and wonderfully made; you are one of a kind. Don't try to conform to be like everyone else. Dare to be the real you. God cannot bless the path of a false person. He knows who He created, so as a spouse, help with this process by knowing each other's likes and dislikes. Find yourselves within yourselves.

Chapter 27

Embrace the Journey and Process

Quick Story:
Recognizing and Embracing the Journey

When I first came home from prison this time around, I noticed that some of the same tests or temptations were still present in my life. The difference now is that I understand the journey and I see things in slow motion. Those same obstacles that tripped me up before, I see them coming, so it allows me to embrace them and understand them. One wrong decision can put you right back at square one, so embrace the journey, one good decision at a time.

The New Man Principle #27:
Embrace the Journey and the Process

1 Peter 1:7 says, "That the trial of your faith, being more precious than gold that perishes, though it is tested with fire, might be found unto praise and honor and glory at the appearing of Jesus Christ".

This journey of transformation is precious. You will see yourself changing and evolving into a new creature but be sure to embrace it. Embrace the new you. Use every lesson, every mistake, every trial, to your benefit.

Had I not embraced this process, I wouldn't have the passion to write to you today. However, part of my journey is to share this information with you so that you may transform through learning and growing. No, it will not be easy, but if you embrace the journey, it starts to become easier because you are locked in. "Though you may stumble," **Psalms 37:24** says, "though he may stumble, he will not fall, for the Lord upholds him with His hand". You see, your help becomes different when you trust the Lord; He will not allow you to fall. So, though this process might be scary, embrace it. You do have help.

Steps to Embracing the Journey

1. **Acknowledge the Process:** Recognize that transformation is a journey with difficulties. Embrace each step as part of your growth.
2. **Stay Positive:** Maintain a positive mindset, even in the face of adversity. Trust that God is guiding you through the process.
3. **Celebrate Small Wins:** Again, celebrate each small victory along the way. These wins build momentum and keep you motivated. (Repeat this step often).
4. **Learn from Mistakes:** Use mistakes as opportunities for growth. Reflect on what you can learn from each experience.

5. **Stay Committed:** Stay committed to your transformation journey, even when it gets tough. Trust that God is with you every step of the way.

The Impact of Embracing the Journey

Embracing the journey allows you to navigate life's challenges with resilience and grace. It helps you stay focused on your goals and maintain a positive outlook, even in difficult times. By understanding and accepting the process, you can transform your perspective and experience greater fulfillment.

The Benefits of Embracing the Process

1. **Personal Growth:** Embracing the journey fosters personal growth and development.
2. **Resilience:** It builds resilience, teaching you to bounce back from setbacks.
3. **Wisdom:** You gain wisdom from your experiences, which helps in making better decisions in the future.
4. **Fulfillment:** There's a deep sense of fulfillment in knowing you are becoming the best version of yourself.

NOTE TO SPOUSE:

Support your spouse by embracing the journey together. Celebrate each other's achievements and stay motivated through challenges. Maintain a positive outlook and trust that God is guiding you both. Remember that transformation is a marathon, and your support is crucial in navigating the ups and downs. You are in this together, and understanding is one of your best weapons.

Chapter 28

The Power of No

The New Man Principle #28: The Power of No

Quick Story:
The Importance of Saying No (Proverbs 2:6)

When I first came home, a friend of mine needed my knowledge and gift in a situation. However, for me to come through for him, it would have put me and my family in a tough spot. So, I delayed the answer.

By the time he had heard back from me, he had figured it out. Not to go into detail but the outcome was extremely negative had I said yes, it would have jammed me up, and I could not afford that this early on in my transformation phase.

The last time I took on a yes for a friend, it led to my downfall, and it took me years to recover. Do not do that to yourself at this point. One of the ways you can master saying no is to run everything by your spouse; they will definitely help you say no. If they're anything like my wife, trust me, no is the answer.

The New Man Principle #28: Learn the Power of No

This principle was probably one of the toughest ones for me because I am a very giving person who loves to help others. However, on this journey, I learned that I can't help everybody. The problem with not saying no is that it will have you fighting battles that don't belong to you. You have to master this principle.

One way to do it is to pray about whom to help, when to help, and most importantly, when to step out of the way or out of a situation. In some cases, you help even when you can't afford to, but it's draining you, and one day you will feel bitter about helping so many people because you're never able to depend on those same people.

Well, ask yourself: how can you depend on those who always need help in the first place? An old man once told me, Son, the helper has to help himself and you help yourself by saying "NO" when it's necessary. Say it with confidence understanding your boundaries.

Steps to Mastering the Art of Saying No

1. **Prioritize Your Well-Being:** Consider your well-being and that of your family before committing to help others.
2. **Pray for Guidance:** Seek God's guidance in deciding when to help and when to step back. Trust that He will lead you in the right direction.
3. **Delay Your Response:** Take time to think before

agreeing to help. This prevents impulsive decisions that may lead to inconvenience.

4. **Set Boundaries:** Establish clear boundaries for yourself and communicate them to others. Be firm in maintaining these boundaries.
5. **Practice Saying No:** Practice politely declining requests. Be honest and respectful in your refusal.

The Impact of Saying No

Learning to say no allows you to focus on your priorities and avoid unnecessary stress. It helps you maintain balance and ensures that you are not overwhelmed by others' demands. Saying no can be empowering and lead to a healthier, more fulfilling life.

NOTE TO SPOUSE

Help your spouse master the art of saying no by intervening when necessary. Encourage open communication and support each other in setting and maintaining boundaries. Understand that saying no is essential for maintaining balance and focus in your lives. Together, you can create a healthy, supportive environment.

Chapter 29

Understanding Your Gifts and Talents

The New Man principle #29: Understanding Your Gifts and Talents

Quick Story:
Discovering My Gift

In prison, I found myself teaching every chance I got. During this time, I realized that I was graced for this gift and that I had a natural inclination to understand and explain concepts. This realization changed my life for the better. Through counsel from godly leaders, I discovered my passion for teaching. This understanding made me recognize that teaching is one of my gifts, along with the gift of faith.

The New Man Principle #29:
Understanding Your Gifts and Talents

Proverbs 18:16 says, "A man's gift maketh room for him, and bringeth him before great men".

Once you understand this principle, the struggle to start a business or determine what to do with yourself will be over. We all have gifts and talents, but not everyone knows how to identify them.

Yet we spend most of our time doing what we see others do and we are not tapped into what we are graced to do. We were created in a special and unique way with gifts and talent that others do not have vs versa.

Be sure through it all you learn what your gifted and talented to do and start doing it. Once you start doing this things become easier for you.

Discovering Your Gift

1. **Reflect on Your Interests:** Understanding what you like to do can be a key indicator of your gifts. For me, I discovered my gift of teaching by recognizing my natural inclination to explain and teach others.
2. **Seek Confirmation:** Sometimes, others can see our gifts more clearly than we can. Seek counsel from godly leaders or those who know you well. They can provide insight and confirmation about your talents.
3. **Observe Your Passions:** Your passions are often aligned with your gifts. Pay attention to what activities make you feel fulfilled and energized. This will help you pinpoint your natural talents.
4. **Pray for Revelation:** Ask God to reveal your gifts to you. He has a purpose for each of us, and understanding your

gifts is a step towards fulfilling that purpose.

Using Your Gifts for Your Purpose

Romans 12:6 says, “Having then, gifts differ according to the grace that is given to us”.

There is a grace that you activate when walking in your correct gift. Once you discover your gift, use it for your purpose.

For example, as a teacher, I use my understanding to help others learn and grow. This brings a sense of fulfillment and aligns with God’s plan for my life.

Benefits of Using Your Gifts

1. **Fulfillment:** Operating in your gift brings a sense of fulfillment and purpose.
2. **Influence:** Your gift can make room for you and bring you before great men, expanding your influence.
3. **Grace:** There is a special grace that accompanies you when you operate in your gift.
4. **Impact:** Using your gifts allows you to make a positive impact on others and fulfill your God-given purpose.

NOTE TO SPOUSE

As a spouse, you can participate by helping your partner discover their gifts. Pay attention to what they like and their passions. You know them better than anyone else, and your support in this discovery will be invaluable. This understanding will help your spouse and strengthen your relationship as you both grow and support each other's journey.

Chapter 30

Walking in Your Purpose

The New Man Principle #30: Walking in Your Purpose

Quick Story:

I always wondered why I felt so much different from others; it was because I was out of purpose. I was living a life according to my environment. Once I found out that I didn't belong in the streets, I was able to walk in my actual calling.

During my last prison bid, I really embraced the call and preached and taught throughout my entire sentence. That's when I felt most fulfilled. If you're wondering why you feel out of place, it's because you are. Align with your real self and be the best version of you, and Heaven will smile upon you. You don't even know how powerful you are, but you will after following these principles. You will transform your life for the better. Likewise, you got this.

The New Man Principle 30: Walking in Purpose

Isaiah 43:2– "When you pass through the waters, I will be with you; and when you pass through the rivers, they will not sweep over you. When you walk through the fire, you will not be burned; the flames will not set you ablaze".

This principle represents fulfillment, godly purpose, and a purposeful lifestyle. It's about doing what you were called to do. When you wake up walking in His perfect will, you experience fullness of joy and a peace that surpasses all understanding.

Walking in purpose means doing what you love to do, something you would do for free because it's in you. My gift of teaching allows me to write this book. I am walking in my gift, and my teaching spirit made this process easier than I could imagine. Had I not followed these principles and discovered my gift, I'd still be lost—maybe sitting in prison or, worse, dead in the streets. I would have never had the chance to become who God has called me to be.

There will be setbacks but keep going. There will be moments when it seems you can't continue. That's when you get on your knees, cry out to God, get up, and keep moving. The late great Dr. King said it best: "If you can't run, walk. If you can't walk, crawl. But don't stop moving".

Transformation is tough, but necessary for all who are living in darkness. The God of all grace will keep you in this process. Walking in your gift and purpose brings you into alignment with who you are meant to be. It is the key to living a fulfilled and meaningful life.

NOTE TO SPOUSE:

Continue to remind your spouse of who they are by affirming them every chance you get. Help them walk this journey out. This, in turn, will help you as you get the best version of the new man. Enjoy life at its highest level. Real transformation starts now and lasts for the rest of your life.

Let's take back everything the devil thought he stole. Transform your life and give back to others who may need what you have to give. Destroying cycles is how we change the world.....

To be continue.......

The New Man Generation Inc.

Instagram: @Josephking2 @Thenewman954

YouTube: @JosephKing919

Email: thenewmangeneration.org

@Faith and Power Church

@Colossia Butts

@Mobile Virtuous Phlebotomy

Made in the USA
Columbia, SC
09 June 2025

59064100R00083